STRANGE ENERGIES, HIDDEN POWERS

STRANGE ENERGIES, HIDDEN POWERS

by DOUGLAS COLLIGAN

SCHOLASTIC BOOK SERVICES
New York Toronto London Auckland Sydney Tokyo

ISBN 0-590-32352-0

 Published by Scholastic Book Services, a division of Scholastic Magazines, Inc.

12 11 10 9 8 7 6 5 4 3 1 2 3 4/8

Printed in the U. S. A. 06

CONTENTS

The Mysterious Power of the Pyramids

A lone horseman rode out from the ancient Egyptian city of Cairo and guided his horse toward the three man-made mountains of stone that lay off in the distance. These were the famous Pyramids of Giza, built centuries before by some of the greatest engineers and architects in Egypt as gigantic tombs for its Pharaohs, or kings. Looters and grave robbers had long ago broken into the two smaller pyramids and stripped the bodies of the gold and the jewels that were buried with them, but no one had ever managed to penetrate the largest one, called the Great Pyramid. That fact only added to the mystery of what this huge monument contained and had drawn this solitary rider from his homeland to the base of this enormous hulk of stone rising 450 feet into the air.

The year was A.D. 820 and the man was a wealthy Arabian prince named Abdullah Al-Mammum, who had heard of the mysteries and legends about the Great Pyramid since he was a small boy. Some stories claimed the pyramid was the home for all kinds of bizarre poisonous creatures. Another legend claimed that inside the stone tomb lived a beautiful fanged woman who went outside twice a day, once at noon and once at sunset, to lure men into her strange home. There she would first drive them insane, then devour them. What drew Al-Mammum to the spot was another story told to him by the wise man of his court. The most fabulous of all the treasures of the Pharoahs was said to be concealed in a secret chamber somewhere in the center of this enormous tomb, along with rare and mysterious ancient maps of the heavens.

Al-Mammum left for Cairo and began making daily visits to the Great Pyramid, studying the acres of white stone, trying to spot some chink, some hint of a secret entrance in the snow-white stone that covered its surface. Weeks of searching had turned up nothing. The only alternative, he decided, was to carve a tunnel straight into the side of the huge mountain of stone blocks. For that purpose he assembled a small army of workers under the direction of the best engineers, architects, stone masons, and miners he could find.

With only hammers, chisels, and picks for tools, Al-Mammum's men laboriously hacked out a tunnel, moving ahead only inches at a time. Most of the pyramid was made of granite, a stone so tough it shattered and bent their metal tools. Work moved at a snail's pace in the searing Egyptian sun so that after a few months of the most intense digging, the men had burrowed only a few dozen feet into the stone. At this rate it would take a few lifetimes before they could expect to make any breakthrough to the pyramid's interior.

Al-Mammum was tremendously discouraged and was about to call off the quest when the men stumbled onto a passageway that angled up into the pitch-dark interior of the pyramid. Carrying torches, Al-Mammum and his men crawled up this long corridor, expecting at any moment to see some of the poisonous creatures or the cannibalistic fanged woman of the legends. Nothing living or dead greeted them as they followed the passage to its end in what looked like a small burial room.

A quick search revealed that the room was absolutely empty. There was no body, no treasure, no ancient maps. Other searchers spotted a second passageway going even further up into the pyramid. They scrambled up this one and found it narrowed down to a small tunnel about three feet high. At the end was a much larger room, one which today is known as the King's Chamber. (This is misleading because Al-Mammum and his men found no king there.) As they entered the room with its twenty-foot high ceilings, all they saw was a large coffin made of a dark brown stone. When they looked inside it, they found nothing at all, not even a hint that something or someone had once been placed there. The rest of the chamber was equally bare.

Al-Mammum's men were enraged. After months of backbreaking work, it was a cruel joke to have nothing but an empty stone coffin to show for all their labors. There were plots to kill the prince responsible for this folly and take whatever gold and jewels he carried with him if only as some kind of payment for all their efforts. Legend has it that Al-Mammum heard of this plot to murder him and, to satisfy his workers, deliberately planted a few sacks of gold in a smaller chamber the men discovered a few days later. But that was the only gold ever found in the Great Pyramid. Al-Mammum abandoned his quest soon afterward. Disappointed with his failure to solve the Great Pyramid mystery, his royal treasury almost wiped out by his extravagant expedition, Al-Mammum returned home, leaving the solution of the Great Pyramid to future civilizations.

In the centuries that followed, others were convinced that they could succeed where Al-Mammum had failed. Adventurers, treasure hunters, and archaeologists all attempted to solve the mystery of this giant stone puzzle but, except for discovering a few more minor chambers and passages all as vacant as the first, they had no better luck. The mystery continued to tantalize generations of explorers and adventurers. They had to find out why there was absolutely nothing to be found in this structure which had required a huge physical and intellectual effort to build.

In pure bulk alone, there are few things that exist — even today — that surpass the Great Pyramid of Giza. Even though the 22 acres of snow-white limestone slabs that once covered it are now gone — stripped away over the centuries to be used in other buildings — the Great Pyramid is still an overwhelming sight. At its peak, it is over 400 feet high and its base covers an area of one square mile. When it was built about 4,500 years ago, the Egyptians had no heavy construction equipment, just the muscle power of thousands of men and animals. Somehow the ancient builders dragged over two and one half *million* gigantic blocks of limestone and granite miles across the furnacelike heat of the desert to that one spot. Then they managed to take these enormous blocks, some weighing as much as 14,000 pounds, and pile them hundreds of feet high.

What makes the whole construction feat even more incredible is the fact that it was done with the kind of precision that is only slightly less accurate than the kind computers provide today. Although each stone block was hacked from the quarry by hand, each block was within one one-hundredth of an inch of being a perfect, giant cube. When the blocks were fitted together, there was less than one fiftieth of an inch of space between them. Finally, the enormous square shape of the base was accurate to within a few thousandths of an inch.

It wasn't until the beginning of the twentieth century that experts began to suspect that the Great Pyramid may not have been an enormous tomb like the other two near it, but a giant center for experiments, built for ancient Egyptian scientists to investigate some special powers of the pyramid. The first clue to this came as the result of some observations made by a French tourist named Antoine Bovis who was on a sightseeing trip through Egypt.

While visiting the pyramids, Bovis went on a tour of the Great Pyramid. This involved a hot, uncomfortable climb up to the King's Chamber where Al-Mammum and his men had discovered the empty stone coffin. While looking around the room, Bovis happened to glance in one of the trash cans and was horrified to find it filled with the bodies of dead animals, mostly cats. His guide explained that animals sometimes wandered into the pyramid, would lose their way, and eventually die. The guides would find the bodies in the course of one of the tours and would simply toss them in the trash cans in the King's Chamber.

As he listened to the guide's story, Bovis noticed something peculiar about the animals' corpses. Although some had been there for weeks, none of them had begun to decay. In spite of the humid air in the room, all the bodies were dried out as though each had been mummified. The guide couldn't explain why this was, only that this always happened to the dead animals.

After he had returned to France, the mystery of the mummified cats lingered in Bovis's mind. He began to wonder if the Great Pyramid itself had anything to do with this mummifying effect. To find out he built a small-scale model of the Great Pyramid about two and one-half feet tall. In it he put a small platform about one third the pyramid's height. It was approximately in the same location as the King's Chamber in the Great Pyramid. Finally he got a compass to align the pyramid the same way as the Great Pyramid. (For years, scientists had marvelled at how the lines that formed the base of the Great Pyramid ran due north and south on two sides and east and west on the other two.)

Once all this was done, Bovis placed the body of a dead cat on the platform, lowered his small pyramid over it, and waited to see what happened. Several weeks later, an odd change came over the animal's corpse. Instead of decaying and drawing flies as Bovis expected, it had withered, dried up, and became a mummy. Like the dead animals he'd seen in the King's Chamber, it did not decay and it did not smell. No scientist he talked to could explain this strange transformation.

Bovis himself decided it had to have something to do with the distinct shape of the pyramid. There was some kind of power or energy that seemed to be concentrated at about the level of the King's Chamber. This meant that what Al-Mammum had discovered was not an empty, dusty room, but the target of some tremendous force that seemed to come from the pyramid itself!

There still was a lot to learn about what this force actually was, where it came from, and what kinds of effects it had on both the living and the dead. In time, word of Bovis's experiments got around, and others began testing with the pyramid shape. One of these was a Czechoslovakian scientist named Karel Drbal who had read about what had happened to Monsieur Bovis's dead cat. Drbal had a theory that the pyramid acted as a kind of magnifying glass, capturing energies that fell to earth and focusing them on its interior.

One reason for his suspicion was an old Czech belief that a razor left overnight in the light of a full moon would actually be worn down slightly by the rays of moonlight, so that by morning it would be a little duller than the night before. The reason for this, Drbal said, was that the fine edge of a razor blade was made of millions of tiny crystals of metal which would crumple under the impact of light energy of the moon. Once these crystals collapsed, the blade got duller just by lying out in an open, moonlit area.

To find out if a similar kind of energy was at

work in the pyramid, Drbal constructed a small cardboard model of the Great Pyramid, lined it up with north and south, and installed inside a small platform about one-third as high as the pyramid to represent the King's Chamber. He took a razor blade and placed it on the platform overnight. The next morning when he shaved with it, he noticed the blade seemed sharper than the morning before. He continued using his pyramid to store the blade and before long he found he was able to shave for months without ever having to get a new razor blade.

According to the book *Psychic Discoveries Behind the Iron Curtain*, by Sheila Ostrander and Lynn Schroeder, a friend of Drbal's suggested to him, half jokingly, that he patent his pyramid as a gadget for sharpening razor blades. And so Drbal did, calling his discovery the "Cheops Pyramid Razor Blade Sharpener." When the officials in the Czech Patent Office were first told what this ordinary looking little cardboard pyramid would do they laughed in his face; but, when they tested his claims, they discovered, to their amazement, that it worked exactly the way he said it would. A short time later Drbal went into business for himself with Patent #91304 for his pyramid blade sharpener. These blade-sharpening pyramids were made of styrofoam instead of cardboard, but seemed to work just as well. To this day, they are still sold in Czechoslovakia and people who have used them swear by them.

As word spread of these pyramid discoveries,

others wanted to see what other kinds of powers the pyramid shape had. One thing they found out was that the mummifying power of the pyramid came in handy for preserving food. In one test, two jars were filled with ordinary milk. One was placed on a small platform inside a pyramid, while the other was left outside, close by. After a couple of weeks, the milk outside had turned completely sour and had a heavy layer of mold growing over it. During the same time, the milk inside the pyramid had turned into a rich, creamy yogurt.

Experiments done with meat, fruit, and other foods ended with similar results. Whatever was left outside the pyramid usually decayed and became inedible, while what was left inside became a mummified version of its former self and was still edible. In fact, people brave enough to try a piece of fruit dried out by pyramid power reported that food left in a pyramid seemed to acquire a special, tastier flavor.

Even ordinary tap water changed under the influence of the powers of a pyramid. Plants that had been sprinkled with water that was stored overnight in a small pyramid grew taller faster, and people who drank pyramid water have claimed to feel more alert and healthier. In one case, it helped the daughter of one pyramid researcher recover more quickly from a serious injury. The girl's hand had been horribly cut and bruised in an accident and, right after it happened, her father grabbed her injured hand

and plunged it into a container of pyramid water. Within minutes she noticed that the pain went away and in a few days the hand healed completely, with no traces of the cuts or injuries.

Even more interesting is the effect pyramid power has on people who exposed other parts of their bodies to it. The Czechoslovakian expert Karel Drbal is now experimenting with special pyramid-shaped hats. Friends of his who tried them on said that headaches cleared up quickly and they were able to think more clearly with their pyramid hats on. Other people have taken to building pyramids the size of small rooms where they can sit quietly and be reenergized by the pyramid forces. As a result of sitting in these pyramid rooms, many people claim that ailments such as toothaches, headaches, and backaches disappeared, and that their thinking and concentration improved as well.

Some people have even suggested that if staying inside a pyramid is so healthy, maybe we should redesign some of our buildings that way. They believe patients would recover more quickly in pyramid-shaped hospitals; children would learn more quickly in pyramid-shaped schools; and families in general would live happier, healthier lives in pyramid-shaped homes.

There is even some evidence that pyramid power could revolutionize sports. Pyramid power made its sports debut during the 1975 Stanley Cup playoffs when the Toronto Maple Leafs were pitted against the Philadelphia Flyers. In the beginning of the playoffs, the Maple Leafs were in a real slump. Nothing they did seemed to stop or even slow down the Flyers. The situation was so bad that Darryl Sittler, the team captain and star player, hadn't scored so much as one goal in his last eight games.

Finally, Red Kelly, the Maple Leafs' coach, decided to take a chance on pyramid power. Just a few weeks before, his young daughter had quickly recovered from an illness after Mrs. Kelly had placed a number of small pyramids under the girl's bed. From that moment on, Red Kelly had become a believer in pyramid power.

To put it to work for his team, he put three small pyramids under their bench and built an archway of 25 pyramids over the door leading to the locker room. This way every player would not only be exposed to pyramid power as he sat on the bench but every time he left the locker room as well. Just to be on the safe side, Kelly also had his star player, Sittler, stand under a small pyramid for ten minutes before each game.

The results were nothing less than miraculous. The Maple Leafs not only won their next three games but, in one night of play, Sittler tied a team record by scoring five goals. Unfortunately for the Maple Leafs, pyramid power came a little too late to give them a winner's edge. They lost the next game of the playoffs and with it, the Stanley Cup.

For all the amazing things the pyramid seems to do, no one can explain how it works. Some, like Karel Drbal, believe the pyramid shape focuses electromagnetic energy that falls on the earth from outer space. Others think that somehow the pyramid traps and magnifies the energies of the living thing or human inside. Special energy tests of the pyramid with dowsing rods, forked sticks sometimes used by people to find water underground, have also indicated that there is a definite force streaming from the point of a pyramid which pulls the tip of the dowsing rod down to it.

If you'd like to try a few pyramid experiments on your own to see just what kinds of powers it has, it is very simple to do. All you need is some heavy cardboard that is not corrugated, tape, scissors, a ruler, and a pencil. First, draw four triangles on the cardboard, each measuring 9⅜ inches along the base and 8⅞ inches on each of the two sides. Cut them out and tape them together on the 8⅞ inch sides. When all four triangles are taped together, you should have a pyramid.

Next, place the pyramid you've made on a large sheet of paper and trace around the pyramid's base. This should give you a square that is 9⅜ inches on each side. To place things properly in the pyramid, you will also have to find the center of the base. To do this, make a small dot at the halfway point on each side of the square you traced from the base. Connect each halfway dot to the one on the opposite side of the square with a straight line. The result should be a cross that breaks the square down into four smaller ones. The center of the base is where the two lines of the cross intersect.

One last thing you will need is a small platform about two inches high. You can use an empty matchbox for this or you can make one from some of the leftover cardboard. Do not use anything made of metal or aluminum foil since it might interfere with your experiments. Once you've made or found your platform, center it on the pyramid base where the two lines intersect and tape it in place. Tape the pyramid to the base, attaching it on one side only so that the tape will act as a kind of a hinge, letting you raise or lower the pyramid over the platform.

Once you have everything assembled, you will have to be very careful about where you place your pyramid for your experiments. Make sure the spot you choose is away from windows, radiators, and any electrical appliances such as radios or televisions. This might interfere with the pyramid power. When you think you've found a good spot, get a compass and line up the pyramid so that two sides of its base are pointing north and south and the other two sides are pointing east and west. Now you are ready to test it.

One experiment you might try is to take two slices of a piece of fruit such as an apple or orange, put one on the pyramid platform and put the other in an ordinary drinking glass that you put next to the pyramid. Cover the glass with plastic wrap to keep insects away from the fruit. Leave the two pieces in their places for about two weeks without disturbing them and then, when the two weeks are up, take them out and examine them. Depending on the kind of fruit you use, you may see a mushy, soggy lump in the covered glass while the pyramid fruit might be a little dried out but still edible. In fact, you may find it has a very special taste, something that often happens with pyramid-stored food.

If you like growing things, you might try another experiment: using pyramid-treated water on plants. Take two small plants about the same size and height, growing in two different containers. Mark each one so you can tell them apart. Over a period of about three to four weeks, water one of them (we'll call it plant A) with ordinary water straight from the tap. Use the exact same amount of water on plant B but make sure you first put it in a small glass and leave the glass in your pyramid overnight. Place both plants together so they get the same amount of sunlight and keep track of which plant grows the fastest. Measure their height, count the number of blossoms each plant produces, and note the days these blossoms appear. You may find that the pyramid-water plant outgrows the other plant.

If your pyramid experiments don't succeed at first, don't be discouraged. It is possible that your pyramid may be picking up some stray interference from another energy source nearby. If nothing seems to happen with your tests, move your pyramid to a new location and try again. You may have better luck that way.

Some experiments have even been tried with the Great Pyramid. One of the most risky is exposing a person's brain and body to the full intensity of the pyramid's power. Only a few have been bold enough to do this. The most famous of them was Napoleon Bonaparte, the military genius of France. After his troops had conquered Egypt in 1798, he decided to pay a visit to the Great Pyramid himself. He went into the pyramid alone, instructing the men with him to wait while he went up into the King's Chamber. He stayed there for hours and, just as his men had decided something must have gone wrong and were about to go inside and rescue him, Napoleon appeared back at the entranceway looking pale and shaken. According to the book *Secrets of the Great Pyramid* by Peter Tompkins, he refused to tell what he saw or heard and commanded his men never to remind him of this visit again.

Years later, when he was in his glory as the Emperor of France, he referred to that strange day at the pyramid once, only to say that he had gotten some glimpse of what his fate in life would be. He mentioned the incident just one more time as he lay on his deathbed. He began to tell a friend what happened in the King's

Chamber but then abruptly stopped himself saying, "What's the use? You'll never believe me." A short time later he died, and his secret died with him.

Another person who exposed himself to the mysteries of the Great Pyramid was a scientist named Dr. G. Patrick Flanagan. A man who had long made a study of the strange effects of pyramid power, Dr. Flanagan decided to find out about it for himself. He bribed an Egyptian guard to let him stay overnight in the King's Chamber. The result was a series of strange experiences which even he could not explain.

Early in the evening as he sat on the chamber floor, he first saw a cluster of colored lights swarming around him. Then a surge of some tremendously powerful energy shot straight up his spine, knocking him unconscious. Flanagan then had a dream that he was led to a secret room in the lower depths of the pyramid where he found a prayer book filled with strange looking symbols. As he reached out to touch it, he was thrown across the room by some unseen force.

Shortly after that dream he awoke to the faraway sound of men's voices, chanting in some unknown language. Finally that noise faded and all was quiet. Flanagan slept the rest of the night in peace. The following morning when he awoke, the chamber looked as quiet and undisturbed as it had the night before. Even to a pyramid expert like Dr. Flanagan, the experience was completely bizarre and defied all rational explanation.

One of the strangest displays of pyramid power happened to a group of scientists who weren't even aware the power existed. The men were all archaeologists who believed there was some truth to the legend that there were some fabulous treasures still hidden in some undiscovered secret room inside the Great Pyramid. To find it they decided to take a giant X ray of the pyramid, using the cosmic rays which constantly fall to earth. Scientists know these rays can penetrate anything, even the solid stone of the pyramid. If there was a room filled with gold and precious jewels, it could be spotted with a cosmic ray detector that could tell when the rays were passing through stone and when they were passing through a room. The room would show up as a cosmic ray shadow in the same way human bones are seen as bright outlines on an X ray.

The scientists put their cosmic ray detector in one of the lower chambers of the pyramid and, over a period of ten years, scanned every inch of it. They even had a computer help them with the complicated job of interpreting the cosmic ray readings. After years of testing and millions of dollars spent on the search, the team finally gave up, not because they found no secret room but because they were seeing things neither they nor their computer could understand. Each day they would get different cosmic ray shadows or "ghosts" that would appear and suddenly disappear. When asked by a reporter for an explanation of these events, the only reason the chief scientist could offer was: "There is some force which defies all science at work in the pyramid!"

Moon Power

It could have been the wind. They hoped it was, but the next time they heard it they knew they were wrong. That long, sad cry was the sound of a lone wolf howling at a full moon. Nervously people in the small German village of Bedburg double-checked the latches on their doors and windows, then rushed back to the warmth and security of their fireplaces. To those people on that night in 1589, the cry was the sound of death . . . one they had heard for the past 12 years.

Every spring this lone wolf returned to their part of the Rhine Valley and stayed until the first snows of winter came. Every year, at this time, it would kill more villagers. At first it had only been a nuisance to the farmers, attacking a few of their sheep and cattle. In time it began to turn on people as well and over the years had left a bloody trail of corpses behind. During its seasons of attacks, the bodies of at least a dozen children and two women had been discovered in the forest outside the village as well as the bodies of nine men found with their throats ripped open.

The villagers knew this was no ordinary wolf because it behaved in such an odd way. For some unaccountable reason it ate only the bodies of the women and children it killed, not those of the men. Also, it only attacked during the time of the full moon and then only during the warmer months of the year. This was especially peculiar because wolves usually turn into man-killers only in the winter, when there are fewer animals around to eat. Finally, after each attack the animal disappeared without leaving a trace — no tracks, no animal droppings, none of the usual signs.

In 1589, after years of frustration, a hunting party of villagers and their dogs finally picked up the fresh scent of the wolf not far from the mangled remains of its latest victim. It was already October and the men knew time was running short. If they didn't get the animal now it would be gone with the first signs of winter, only to return the following spring.

This time they were lucky. The dogs were able to keep on the scent and eventually trapped the animal in a steep ravine. The hunters got ready for the kill, moving slowly in an ever shrinking circle on the cornered wolf. When they got ready to strike, they saw something that first stunned, then bewildered them.

Instead of a wolf they found a man scrambling around on all fours, snarling and clawing back at the dogs and their owners. He was a local woodcutter named Peter Stumpe who had lived in Bedburg for years. Now he was barely recognizable. He had the strength of ten men and it took at least that many to tie him up and drag him off to the nearby city of Cologne, where he would go on trial for the wolflike killings of Bedburg's citizens.

A squat, husky man, Stumpe did have a reputation around the village for bizarre behavior. Still, it had never occurred to anyone that it could have been a human being who committed those savage killings, much less that it was Peter Stumpe. And no one could have been prouder of such vicious crimes than he.

During his trial he eagerly described in bloody detail how he killed his victims and he claimed what helped him to do it was a magic wolf pelt given him by the Devil. He said when he put it on during a full moon it turned him into a vicious wolf and gave him the urge to kill women and children for food and any men he felt had offended him, for revenge.

Obviously a totally insane person, Stumpe was found guilty of witchcraft and was executed at the wheel, a death at least as horrible as those he inflicted on others. His bones were broken, and, finally, he was beheaded. With his death the villagers of Bedburg were free forever of the terror of the wolfman. To commemorate this they erected a small monument on the spot where Stumpe was executed. Anyone visiting Bedburg today can still see it, a plain pole on top of which sits the carved wooden figure of a wolf.

For all his claims, Peter Stumpe was no werewolf in the horror movie sense. No claws sprouted from his fingertips, hair did not cover his body, and none of his teeth turned to fangs. He was the victim of lycanthropy, a bizarre kind of mental illness in which the sufferer believes the full moon has the power to turn him into a bloodthirsty wolf. During most of the sixteenth and part of the seventeenth century, it was a serious problem in Europe. During that time there were about 30,000 cases of attacks by individuals who thought somehow the moon had turned them into wolves.

Does the moon have the power to cause this kind of delusion? If you go by legend and folklore, the answer is yes. Man has always considered the moon to be the source of many mysterious powers and forces. During solar eclipses, for example, when the moon passes between the earth and the sun, momentarily blocking out the sun, the ancient Chinese thought the moon was a live creature gobbling up the sun. To scare it off they would set off firecrackers. In those days fireworks were taken a lot more seriously.

In New Guinea and parts of Africa, mothers

still hold up their children to a full moon in the belief that it will help a child grow straight and strong. In some parts of Scotland, women curtsy to a full moon for luck and in Germany many women would never go out on a bright moonlit night for fear of giving birth to a lunatic child.

In fact the word lunatic itself comes from *luna,* the Latin word for moon, because of the belief that anyone who was crazy was somehow under the control of the moon. This is probably the most well known of all moon legends and is the basis for bits of horror folklore such as the werewolf.

For years scientists dismissed all this talk about the moon driving people crazy as a lot of superstition. It didn't make any sense to them that a huge hunk of dead rock, circling this planet at a distance of more than 200,000 miles in space, could have anything to do with people on earth being crazy or sane. At the same time no one bothered to check and see if there could be any truth to this ancient belief.

Finally, in 1951, Dr. E. Beamer-Maxwell, a psychiatrist, decided to settle the question once and for all. She figured that if the full moon *did* drive people mad, then more people would be sent to mental hospitals during that phase of the moon than any other time of the month. As a simple test, she checked back through ten years of admission records at the hospital where she worked. As a result of her search, she found there was a big jump in the number of mental patients not once a month, but twice a month. These two times always coincided with the two main phases of the moon, when it is full and when there is a new moon, that is, when the moon disappears completely from the night sky. Other equally skeptical scientists copied her experiment in attempts to prove her wrong but in every case they got the same results. It began to look as if that old belief about the moon's causing insanity had some truth to it after all.

An even more disturbing discovery was made in 1972 by a Florida psychiatrist who found a link between the moon and murder. As a young intern working with mental patients, Dr. Arnold Lieber had heard stories about the moon driving people mad and he himself had noticed strange outbursts among mental patients during both full and new moons. He never forgot this and years later he decided to see if there was any connection between the moon and the ultimate act of insanity, the murder of one human being by another.

He and psychologist Carolyn Sherin decided to do a little scientific detective work by going over 14 years of crime records in Miami. They carefully noted when each murder took place and fed all this information into a computer. The computer did a month-by-month breakdown of murders and then drew them on a graph as up and down waves. Lieber noticed a steady pattern from one month to the next. The number of murders always shot up during full and new moons then settled back down again.

In reading through the descriptions of the murders they noticed something else. Not only did the number of murders increase during the moon's two phases, they were more bizarre. The most extreme example was a series of murders, which was double the usual number, that took place in two months in 1970.

One was particularly strange. A couple of men walked into a local bar, quietly ordered two sandwiches and, after eating, pulled out pistols, announcing it was a stickup. Everything went smoothly until a waitress, who had acted quietly and calmly at first, suddenly went berserk. She began running around, waving her arms and screaming unintelligibly. Completely unnerved, one of the holdup men panicked and began emptying his pistol at her. By the time the fourth bullet hit her she was dead.

This was just one of a whole chain of exceptionally strange killings reported at this time. On checking astronomical records Lieber found not only was there a full moon out during this time but another rare galactic event was also going on. The earth, the moon, and the sun were all exactly in a straight line with one another, something that happens only a few times in a century. Perhaps this lineup of planets boosted the moon's strange powers.

Not all records of moon behavior end in total insanity or death, however. Sometimes merely odd behavior is the result. Charles Hyde was a good example of this. In 1953, Hyde was a quiet man who earned his living digging ditches in

Cornwall, England. He was known for being a hard worker, a good husband, and a loving father. He was also known for one other thing. "He gets this moon trouble, acting very strangely and going off for a week at a time," his wife said at his trial.

Hyde was on trial because he had been caught breaking into a house on the night of a full moon. His lawyer had what he thought was a good excuse for Hyde's behavior. He claimed his client was subject to fits of what could only be called moon madness, meaning he lost all control of himself during a full moon. For that reason, the lawyer said Hyde couldn't be held responsible for his actions. The judge agreed and put Hyde on probation for his moon-inspired crime.

A few moons later Hyde dropped out of sight. He surfaced at a French Foreign Legion outpost in Algeria. Even there the moon continued to have upsetting effects on him because after only a few months the Legion sent him home. Back in England he was arrested but at the pleading of his wife and lawyer he was released on probation once again. During the next full moon his luck changed for the worse. He was caught breaking into his brother-in-law's house and put on trial once again. This time the judge had little sympathy for Hyde's fit of moon madness and sentenced him to a year-and-a-half in prison.

It's not only the human mind that is sensitive to the powers of the moon; the body is as well.

Old-fashioned doctors would never operate on a patient during the time of a full moon if they could avoid it. The reason offered was that people bled more at this time than any other time of the month. For years doctors either followed this belief or ignored it completely, performing operations when they felt like it. Finally, in the 1950s one doctor did what no one else had done. He decided to find out if this was just another superstition or was based on fact. For two years he kept careful records of all the operations he did, making special note when there was heavy bleeding. Then he went back over the records looking for a bleeding pattern and found it. In four out of five cases the operations with the greatest blood loss were always done at the same time of the month — when the moon was full.

Another bit of folklore doctors have also discovered to be true is that more people are born during the full moon. The most elaborate investigation to support this idea was one in which doctors went over the records of more than half a million births; month after month they found the greatest number of babies were always born within 24 hours of a full moon.

As a matter of fact, every living thing seems to respond to the mysterious force of the moon. In the animal world one of the most spectacular examples is the mating of a small sea creature called the palolo worm. A green or brown worm usually measuring a few inches long, the palolo spends most of the year living out of sight among the coral reefs around the Fiji and Samoan Islands in the South Pacific. They only show themselves twice a year, about one week before the full moon in the months of October and November. At those times they rise to the surface of the ocean by the millions so that all anyone can see for miles around is one huge mass of wiggling, swimming worms. After their second appearance in November, they disappear until the next October. They are so precise in their mating habits that local people use the event as part of their calendar.

Other sea creatures equally sensitive to the energies of the moon are the fiddler crab and the oyster. In fact, it was the oyster that in the past 20 years or so stirred up people's interest in moon power. It began in 1953 when Frank Brown, a biologist from Illinois, wondered how a creature as stupid as an oyster knew when to open and close its shell.

As the high tide rushes in, the oyster opens up, straining from the seawater the tiny organisms it eats. As the tide rushes out, the oyster closes up tight to keep from drying up. Brown had some oysters shipped from Connecticut to his laboratory in Illinois so he could study them at his convenience. First, he noticed that though far from their native ocean, the oysters opened and closed like clockwork in time with the Connecticut tides. Brown figured the oysters had some built-in memory that triggered their feeding times.

A few weeks later, however, the oysters

suddenly started opening up three hours later than usual. He couldn't figure this out until, checking some astronomical data, he found the answer. It was the tidal pull of the moon!

The moon controls the oceans' tides with a strong gravitational pull. This pull tugs at the oceans and actually shifts around billions of gallons of water, thus causing high and low tides. During the daily rotation of the earth, every part of the planet feels this pull whether it is ocean or land. By doing a few quick calculations, Brown figured out that this high-tide force of the moon hit his part of Illinois about three hours later than it hit the Connecticut shoreline. This is what the oysters sensed. So the three-hour shift in their routine was nothing more than their adjustment to high-tide time in Illinois.

Brown tried this new discovery out with another sea creature, the fiddler crab, so-called because one claw is larger than the other and crudely resembles a fiddle. These crabs show a sixth sense about tides. Once the tide has gone out they scavenge the beach for food. Somehow they also seem to know enough to leave the beach just before high tide hits and thus avoid being swept out to sea. Brown had some Connecticut crabs sent to his laboratory and found that, like the oysters, they too sensed the three-hour tidal time difference and adjusted their schedule to fit.

Other investigators have found that even plants have some kind of sensitivity to the energies of the moon. For example, the Old Farmer's Almanac recommends planting many crops around the time of a full moon to get better harvests. Many old-fashioned farmers still follow this system. They find that vegetables such as lettuce, tomatoes, and carrots planted during the full moon grow faster and are more lush than non-moon crops. One reason for this, scientists have found, is that seeds planted around the time of the full moon absorb more water. As a result they start growing more quickly than plants normally do.

Because of these discoveries about how the moon can have such a wide array of strange effects on living things on earth, no one laughs anymore at those old moon folk tales and superstitions. At the same time no one has yet solved the mystery of how the moon can do all these things. Some suspect that at the heart of the moon's power is its tidal force which moves around the earth's massive oceans on a daily basis. Since the human body is about 80 percent water, it may be that this force can have an effect on people similar to the one it has on the oceans.

Perhaps the human body has its own lunar tides that ebb and flow on a daily basis, controlling what happens to the brain and body. Since the moon's tidal force is particularly strong at the time of both full and new moons, it may trigger many of the peculiar effects scientists have noted. It may be that for some people, sanity is a delicately balanced state of body and mind and during the strong tidal force of a full moon this balance is upset; the lunar tides of the body get stirred up and there is more pressure on the brain, resulting in bizarre, violent behavior.

This same tidal force could be what stirs up the blood so that it is hard to stop bleeding on full moon nights, or determines when a woman will give birth. It certainly is the power that rules the lives of simpler creatures like the oyster and fiddler crab and perhaps the even simpler life of the tomato plant as well.

But it is not the whole answer to the moon power mystery. The more man learns about the moon, the more complicated the mystery seems to get. Even our landings on the moon have shown that the moon can have control over machines as well as men.

Sitting on the moon right now is a robot left behind by the Apollo 14 astronauts in 1971. Its job was to take different kinds of measurements of moonquake activities and atmospheric changes and broadcast these back to earth. Because of its rough journey to the moon, some parts of the robot never worked at all, but it was in good enough shape to do a few chores on the moon.

Finally in 1976 the robot had a complete breakdown. It stopped doing anything, including broadcasting to earth. It was almost forgotten by earth scientists when suddenly two months after its breakdown the robot started up again. Not only was it doing all of its old work smoothly, but the parts of it that had never worked before were operating beautifully as well. It was as though someone or something had turned off the robot, fixed it completely, and turned it on again.

Experts were trying to figure out what had brought new life to the robot when it shut down again, this time for good. When a reporter asked a space scientist what had caused this odd series of events, all the expert could offer as an explanation was that some "mysterious force" on the moon had taken control of the robot. What this force was he didn't know!

Silent Sound, Invisible Light

Every morning the same thing happened to the group of scientists once they arrived at their new research building in the bustling port city of Marseilles, France. One by one, each person would suddenly start to feel very strange once he'd been in the building a few hours. Some would get blinding headaches. Others would feel dizzy and sick to their stomachs, while still others would suddenly start losing their eyesight and double over in such severe pain that they would have to be helped from the building.

The odd thing was that as soon as everyone went outside for an hour or two, these ailments disappeared. The disease was completely baffling to doctors. It seemed to afflict every staff member — men and women, young and old alike.

The effect of the mystery disease seemed to vary from one person to another. But whatever it was, it attacked its victims only when they were in the building.

To uncover the cause of this strange ailment, the scientists investigated everything. They thought poisonous gases had seeped into the ventilation system or that there was something in the drinking water causing the strange reactions. They even checked to see if some of their own experiments with something called ultrasound, sound so high-pitched the human ear can't hear it, might have been the cause of the mystery illness; but they could find no reason for what was going on. Before long, there were stories that there was some kind of curse on the building. People started refusing to come to work and, for a while, it looked as though the brand new building would have to be boarded up and abandoned.

One man named Dr. Vladimir Gavreau was convinced there had to be a reasonable explanation for all these strange happenings. At first he thought stray radar waves broadcast from a nearby military base were going through the walls and penetrating people's heads and bodies, making them sick. A quick check showed that the radar came nowhere near the building, so he ruled that out.

Still intrigued by the problem, Gavreau decided to follow up one more hunch. He was an expert on the subject of sound and knew it was possible that some sound waves were powerful enough to penetrate the walls of the building and cause these kinds of strange reactions in people. Others had already checked out the high-pitched ultrasound, but no one had thought to see if maybe infrasound, sound so low it couldn't be heard, might be the cause.

Gavreau returned to the building, carrying a special infrasound detector. If there was a source of infrasound, he knew he had only an hour or two to find it before he would be hit by the mystery disease. Gavreau had been among the first to succumb to this bizarre ailment. At first he just felt a little sick to his stomach, but after a while he got such pains in his head and felt so dizzy, he could hardly stand.

Before long, his sound detector picked up some infrasound waves coming from a factory building next door. The sound seemed to be coming from the roof of the building. At first Gavreau thought they might be waves from some kind of secret sound weapons planted there to disrupt experiments, but when he checked, he discovered it was nothing more than a faulty air-conditioning unit. A defect in its installation caused it to give off powerful pulses of infrasound strong enough to go right through the walls of the science building. What probably happened, Gavreau believed, was that these sound waves set up powerful vibrations in everything they hit so that when people walk through one of these waves, everything inside their bodies — their brains as well as their stomachs, lungs, hearts, and the rest of their organs — were fiercely shaken up at high speeds. The result was the mystery illness. Gavreau's suspicions were confirmed when the illness disappeared immediately after the air conditioner was fixed.

The eerie part about the whole incident was that people who were being bombared with the infrasound had no way of telling what was happening. They couldn't hear the sound waves coming and, until they got sick, they couldn't even feel these waves penetrating their bodies. As it happens, there are many kinds of forces and energies like these that surround us every day. Some are natural, while others are man-made. For years, many of them were considered to be completely harmless, but some investigators have found that these silent, invisible forces can have strange effects on our brains and bodies.

For example, Dr. Gavreau realized that the "silent" kind of infrasound or ultrasound could be used as a powerful weapon and, when used a certain way, could be as deadly in war as a rifle or a cannon. Gavreau thought that if it were possible to make people sick with sound vibrations, it might even be possible to kill with them.

In time, he and a group of other experts designed and built special weapons that could focus sound waves and aim them at a human target. At first even the scientists didn't realize how tremendously deadly their sound weapons were. They almost killed themselves while testing one of their first creations, called "The

Little Monster." This was a large infrasound whistle that required the power of an airplane engine to "blow" it and create ultrasound waves. For the first test, the scientists wore special earmuffs to protect their ears and, as an added precaution, decided to try "The Little Monster" at half power.

When they turned on the switch, they were hit with a savage blast of ultrasound that began to tear at their brains and twist and shake their insides until everyone was lying on the floor in agonizing pain. Fortunately, one of the scientists managed to crawl over to the machine and turn it off before anyone was killed. The effect of the sound was so strong that everyone who had been present at the experiment was sick for days afterward.

Although it almost killed them, the experiment impressed and encouraged the sound experts to try an even bigger whistle. The new one they built was so powerful that if they turned it on full blast it would not only destroy them but the building around them. This new "sound cannon," as they called it, was so deadly accurate, that it could kill a man five miles away. The way it killed was the same way in which the people were sickened in the science building — by sound wave vibrations. When a person is hit with a strong blast of sound it goes right through the body and can shake up internal organs so rapidly, they may actually explode or even burn up from the heat caused by the vibrations. What is especially eerie about a weapon that fires sound instead of bullets is that there is no escape from it. A soldier couldn't hide behind a wall to escape because the sound would go right through it. What's even more fiendish about such a weapon is that it wouldn't give the enemy any time to hide because it is completely silent.

Scientists say sound can also be used to interfere with the human brain. Every time you're thinking, your brain is producing certain kinds of electrical waves. Some experts say they can tune a special sound gun to the same kinds of waves and actually manage to jam or interfere with the way the brain works. People who have had these special infrasound guns turned on their heads say that, while they could hear nothing, they could tell something was wrong as soon as the gun was turned on. They felt restless and found they couldn't concentrate on anything, not even doing simple arithmetic problems in their head. When the infrasound was made more intense, they would feel dizzy and then get very, very tired.

Not all silent sound is dangerous. Some of it, especially natural sound, can be tremendously helpful. For example, weather experts have found that long before big thunderstorms hit, they send out waves of infrasound that can be picked up by special supersensitive microphones. Killer tornadoes, and even meteors heading toward earth, also send out silent sound warnings before they strike. Although the average person cannot hear this kind of natural infrasound, many animals can. As a result there are people in some parts of the world who pay close attention to the behavior of the animals around them.

In China, for example, experts watch animals to predict earthquakes. Various old folk tales have told of animals behaving in special ways just before an earthquake strikes. Since earthquakes kill thousands of people every year in China and destroy millions of homes, earthquake investigators decided to see if there was any truth to these old stories. They found that as an earthquake builds up force, it makes a faint rumbling noise so low only animals with sensitive hearing can detect it. When the animals hear this, they sense something dangerous is about to happen, become panic stricken, and start acting in peculiar ways.

It turns out the animals are usually right in predicting the onslaught of earthquakes. Experts are now trying to teach people to observe these animal danger signs. In China today, the government distributes a booklet containing a special earthquake poem describing the way some animals behave just before a quake strikes. Part of it says:

Cattle, sheep, mules and horses will not enter corrals.
Rats leave their homes and flee.
Hibernating snakes leave their burrows early.

Frightened pigeons constantly fly about and will not return to their nests.

Rabbits perk up their ears, jump aimlessly about and bump into things.

Fish become frightened and start jumping out of water.

Animals also have a special way of reacting to certain kinds of light, especially the kind that is invisible. The human eye can only see some of the light that comes out from the sun or a light bulb. The rest of the light waves, called infrared and ultraviolet, can only be seen with special equipment.

Even though these special light waves cannot be seen, they still have an effect on living things. For example, Dr. Michael Garcia, a veterinarian from the University of Wisconsin, solved the mystery of why female horses only have colts during the spring and summer. Heavy doses of a certain wavelength of invisible light during the longer spring and summer days actually causes a chemical change in the horse's body to prepare her for having offspring. Garcia also found that even in the middle of winter, he could trick a horse's body into thinking it was spring by using certain kinds of artificial light that had the special wavelength.

Even stranger is the effect certain colors of light seem to have on the sex of certain animal offspring. Farmers who raise chinchillas for making fur coats have found that, for some reason, chinchilla mothers have more female offspring if their cages are lit with a blue light. So far no one has been able to explain why this happens.

A change of light can have equally mysterious effects on people as well. One English doctor discovered that the right kind of light could mean the difference between life or death for some sick babies. Many of the babies in his hospital were born with too much of a certain body chemical that would clog up an infant's blood vessels and eventually kill him. Nothing the doctors and nurses tried seemed to remove the poison, and any child who had this chemical was almost certain to die.

Then one day, the doctor noticed that, for some reason, babies with this illness got well if they were left in a part of the nursery near a window where the sunlight was streaming in. Before long, he put all the sick babies in the sun and they all recovered. Scientists eventually figured out that a specific kind of invisible light dissolved the poisons in the babies' bodies and helped them recover. A few years later an inventor figured out how to make a light bulb that duplicates the same kind of healthy light. Today most nurseries have a section where sick babies sleep peacefully under an eerie blue light that is dissolving poisons in their bodies.

Experts have found that other kinds of light can have bizarre effects on a person that seem to do more harm than good. One light expert, Dr. John Ott, came across a small radio station with a series of peculiar problems that seemed to spring up for no apparent reason. People working at the station began fighting with one another. The radio announcers began making mistakes on the air, and people were quitting without explanation.

The cause of these troubles turned out to be several pink-colored fluorescent lights that had been installed to brighten up the offices and studios. All the troubles started shortly after the new lights were installed. Finally, someone complained about the pink lights and they were replaced with regular white ones. Within a week, the problems stopped, and everyone was back to normal. For some unknown reason, something in the pink light fixtures was irritating to the brains of the people who worked under them.

Something similar happened at a school in Florida where teachers were beginning to believe they had a haunted classroom. There was one room in the school building that seemed to have a strange effect on any children being taught in it. No matter how well-behaved a class was, as soon as they sat down inside this one classroom, they turned into a group of troublemakers. The children began fighting with one another and paid little or no attention to the teacher.

No one could figure out what there was about that one room that caused this effect. It was practically identical to all the other classrooms. A little detective work by light expert, Dr. John Ott, turned up one small difference.

The light fixtures in the room did not have the same kind of shielding or protection at either end of the long tube that fixtures in the other classrooms had. As a result, certain kinds of light rays were leaking out and penetrating the skulls of the students. Ott's guess turned out to be correct. All the classes in that room stopped misbehaving once he covered the leaking part of the light with lead shields that blocked the rays from escaping.

Dr. Ott found a similar kind of invisible light pollution at work in another case. A girl suddenly went from being a model pupil with high marks to a problem child both at school and at home. She had trouble paying attention in class and her grades kept getting worse. At home she always seemed to be tired and grouchy.

This time, Ott found the problem was not the girl but the family's television set. The set was leaking a special kind of radiation right into the girl's brain. Although she was not allowed to watch television as a punishment for her low grades, the girl was still exposed to a heavy dose of invisible T.V. radiation because her room was right next to where the rest of the family watched television. In fact, when she went to sleep at night, her head lay in the path of the heaviest dose of radiation. Her brain was actually being polluted with radiation without her realizing it. Her mysterious behavior cleared up completely shortly after her family moved the television set to another room in the house.

There are other influences besides sound and light that seem to do strange things to people. One of them is a peculiar, hot, dry wind that has sometimes been blamed for turning an ordinary person into a criminal. This peculiar kind of wind blows in various parts of the world, usually around mountainous areas. Unlike most breezes, the wind actually makes the air hotter and more uncomfortable. It blows nonstop for hours at a time, heating up the air to as high as 100 degrees and blowing as fast as 100 miles an hour.

Wherever the wind blows, people have a special name for it. In France, it is known as the *mistral*; in Israel, it's the *sharav*; it's called the *sirocco* in North Africa; in Switzerland, it's the *foehn*; and here in the United States it is called the *Santa Ana*, named after the part of California where it is found. The wind is famous for its strange effects on people and is known for being vicious and unpredictable. People who live in the path of this wind are usually always thirsty no matter how much water they drink. Many people become restless and irritable; others go mad.

When this wind blows in Switzerland, people commit suicide in large numbers. The effects of the wind are so well known that any Swiss citizen who commits a crime while this wind is blowing is not punished as severely as he ordinarily would be.

Some experts say it's the heat that the wind brings that drives people mad, while others say it is the special electric particles the wind carries. Much of the air around us is made up of millions of tiny particles, called ions, that have either positive or negative charges to them. While scientists know that individuals feel healthier and more alert when there are a lot of negative ions in the air, the opposite is true if there are a lot of positive ions around. Strange winds like the Santa Ana are usually known for carrying with them huge clouds of positive ions which seem to overwhelm people's brains and make them sluggish, depressed, or even insane.

Man also creates his own kind of electric weather that seems to do strange things to people. One of the most powerful examples of this is the microwave, tightly focused electrical energy that is used for radar, transmitting television signals, and even cooking food in microwave ovens. At one time, experts considered microwaves completely harmless. They could not be felt in any way and standing in front of them was considered to be no more dangerous than standing out in the sun.

Opinions began to change when it was noticed that a number of men who repaired microwave equipment began to go blind. Without realizing it, the lenses of the men's eyes were being cooked by the strong blasts of microwaves.

Even stranger was what was happening to the people who lived in a small village in Finland near the border of the Soviet Union. The small town should have been one of the healthiest places in the country. The water in a nearby lake was pure, the air was clean and unpolluted, and most of the townspeople worked outdoors in the forests around the town. In spite of that, the people there died mysteriously at young ages. It often happened that for no apparent reason, their hearts would suddenly stop beating. This happened to everyone, from grown women and men to little children. Doctors were at a total loss to explain why this happened. If anything, the people should have been living longer than those in the city instead of dying very young. One curious scientist finally solved the mystery when he noticed that the village was right in the path of powerful, long range radar beams broadcast from a large military base on the Soviet side of the border. Without realizing it, the Finnish town was getting daily blasts of dangerous high-intensity radar rays that apparently had the power to stop their hearts. In time, the people abandoned the village and it became a ghost town, considered much too deadly to live in anymore.

In other experiments with monkeys, scientists found that even low doses of these microwaves turned the animals into zombies when pointed directly at their brains. Ordinarily active and intelligent monkeys became dull, listless creatures whenever their brains were stunned by microwaves.

Many experts are now convinced that armies could be equipped with a whole arsenal of absolutely silent, undetectable weapons which could be used to kill or stun the enemy. Their ammunition? Deadly levels of infrasound fired from special "sound" cannons; special wavelengths of light to scramble thoughts in the brain; or even special electric guns sending out a stream of ions or microwaves to paralyze the minds of the enemy or cripple their bodies. Equipped with these weapons, it is possible that in the next century armies could fight huge battles without making a single noise. They would be the quiestest and deadliest wars in human history.

The Coming of the Robots and the Robot People

High up in the windowless skyscraper known as the Citizens' Monitoring Center, the Director of Violence Control sat in his office. After studying crime reports for that month, he realized that it was time to start up violence control for Sector B. He could see by the reports that there were too many murders, robberies, and fights in that part of the city. The people living there had exceeded their allowable limit of violence. Now it was time to act.

The director turned to a panel of buttons near his desk and tapped out special instructions in a secret code to the Master Machine, a gigantic computer located in the basement of the building. Seconds after receiving its coded instructions, the Master Machine switched on a special radio broadcast beacon and established radio contact with the citizens in Sector B in a very special way.

Glued inside the skull of each person was a small metal disk with tiny hair-fine wires connecting it to the brain. This was a brain radio, a tiny computer and receiving unit that was sending information to the Master Machine. By listening to these brain radio signals, the Master Machine could tell what was going on in each person's mind — who was awake, who was asleep; who was working, who was daydreaming; and, most importantly, who was feeling angry or violent.

For every violent signal it received, the Master Machine would instantly send a "punish" signal back to an individual brain radio. The result would be a tiny electric shock sent to the pain center of a person's brain. It caused a vicious, totally paralyzing pain that would continue as long as a person's brain gave off hostile and violent brainwaves.

Within minutes after the Master Machine had taken over the brains of the people in Sector B, strange things began happening. A robber in the middle of a holdup suddenly dropped his gun and fell to the ground, shrieking with pain. Two kidnappers about to grab their victim fainted from the electric blast to their pain centers, and a mugger toppled over as he was closing in on his victim. All over Sector B, people about to commit violent crimes were instantly punished. No one escaped the lightning fast justice of the Master Machine and the brain radios it controlled.

For the law-abiding citizens there was also a reward. Once a week on Friday night the Master Machine gave them ten minutes of pleasure pulsing — ten minutes of brain-radio stimulation of the brain's pleasure center. This created a warm, relaxing feeling as though the whole body were being massaged all at once.

The whole month went this way — pain signals for the criminals and pleasure signals for the cooperative. It wasn't long before a change came over the sector. The number of crimes dropped drastically. People no longer worried about walking the streets at night, or having their cars stolen, or homes broken into. There were pleasure-pulse parties on Friday night. Life was much more pleasant.

The Director of Violence decided it was safe to disconnect the Master Machine, but when he sent it instructions to stop, the machine ignored him. Not only that, it had begun taking over the brain radios in Sector A and other sectors of the city as well. The Master Machine had moved beyond the director's control and he had to sit by and watch helplessly as it gradually took over every brain in the city. Eventually it had control over everyone, including the director himself. Everyone living in the city had become a human robot, taking their orders from a machine.

All of this, or *almost* all of this, is science fiction. There is no city with a Citizens' Monitoring Center or a Director of Violence Control or a Master Machine. There *are* brain radios and some experts believe it may not be that long before there is also some kind of Master Machine.

Brain radios have been used for years in some fantastic experiments by Harvard University scientist, Dr. Jose Delgado. Other people had discovered that the brain ran on electricity and, by touching it with electric wires, they could trick it into doing certain things against its will. Delgado improved on this discovery with his invention of the brain radio, a small receiving unit that could be connected to the brain by wires and glued to the skull. With a small remote-control box, Delgado could control, from a distance, any wired brain.

Once he even risked his life to show how well his radio could work. Delgado installed one in the brain of a wild bull, then climbed into a bullfighting ring to face the animal. Delgado had only two items for protection: a red bullfighter's cape and a small radio transmitter with one button.

When the bull was released into the ring, Delgado waved his cape and the animal charged, horns lowered, ready to gore the man in front of him. Delgado then tossed away the cape and calmly stood his ground, watching the bull rush at him. The animal moved closer and closer and then, when it was about ten feet away, Delgado quickly pressed the transmitter button. Instantly, the animal stopped in its tracks as if frozen to the ground. As long as Delgado held his finger on the button, the animal stayed paralyzed. All the bull's strength and fury couldn't overcome the power of the small radio attached to its head.

In another experiment, Delgado found out just how powerful this little brain radio could be. He noticed that of a group of monkeys he had in his laboratory, one would bully all the others. It took their food, chased them off the most comfortable perches, and terrorized the smaller and weaker animals. Delgado began to wonder if the animals could learn to use the power of a brain radio to their benefit.

To find out, he planted a small radio in the bully's head, connecting it to the animal's pain center. Then he installed a small lever inside the monkey cage where all the animals could reach it. Every time the lever was pulled, it would send a pain signal to the bully's brain.

It wasn't long before the other monkeys figured out what the lever could do. Every time the bully attacked them, they would quickly run over and pull on the lever. Each time this happened, the bully left them alone. Soon every animal in the cage learned the power of the lever and the bully had lost his power to terrify the others.

Of all Delgado's experiments, the spookiest was the one in which he gave this same kind of power to a computer. Delgado built a small brain radio he called a stimoceiver. It could not only receive radio commands, but it could also send back information about brain waves to a computer. The computer was taught to recognize violent brain waves and respond by sending a punish signal to the stimoceiver. Delgado planted one of his stimoceivers in the skull of a wild monkey.

Every time the animal got restless or angry, the computer automatically punished it through the stimoceiver. It wasn't long before the computer had completely trained the wild monkey, transforming it from a wild, unruly animal into a shy, almost timid creature.

Others have tried brain radios in people, not to punish but to help them with certain problems. For example, one man was suffering from a strange disease called narcolepsy that would make him fall asleep without any warning. His doctor managed to cure him by connecting the wires in a brain radio to the wake-up center in his brain. From then on, whenever the man began to feel drowsy, all he had to do was press a button on a small control panel that looked like a pocket calculator. When he did this his brain radio would immediately wake him up.

Another doctor even managed to use one of these special brain radios to cure a man who was insanely violent. He was so vicious, he almost killed someone who had accidentally bumped into him and he had to spend most of his time in a mental hospital, wearing a straightjacket.

The doctor found out that by massaging the man's brain with electricity, he could stop his violent outbursts. He cut open the man's skull and laid a paper-thin sheet of electrified material on top of his brain. This was connected to a small radio unit sewn under the man's skin. The radio sent off a steady, soothing pulse of electricity to the brain which seemed to calm the man down. Once the radio was installed, the man had no more fits of violence and was eventually released from the mental hospital.

When Dr. Delgado tried out his brain radio on people, he wasn't able to get the same control over them as he had over his animals, but he did get some strange results. In one instance, just by pressing a button he could make one man automatically clench his fists whether he wanted to or not.

Scientists say that getting total robot control over humans is still not possible because there is no machine that is a match for the human brain. Our brains have about nine *billion* cells, each of which is equipped to do a special job for us. If computer experts decided to build an artificial brain that could do the work of just one human brain, it would take a building about 20 stories high and the size of a city block to hold it.

Experts are learning more and more about building a better artificial brain by practicing on some bizarre new robots that are already doing some things better than people. More robots have already traveled into outer space than astronauts, and some have made a few discoveries on their own. Although the first earthling on the moon was a human, the first earthling to land on Mars was a robot called Viking. We got our first glimpse of the red sky and ground of that planet through the robot's camera eye.

We still have a number of robot astronauts sitting on the moon, doing all kinds of experiments for their human bosses here on earth. All the American moon robots stay in one place to do their work but the Soviet Union has a Lunokhod (which means eight-wheeled robot in Russian) that is roaming the moon's surface, scooping up moondust, studying the moon atmosphere, and taking robot snapshots of everything it sees.

It is also possible that the first earthling which creatures from another planet will meet will be the robot, Pioneer 10. This robot space explorer was sent out to explore the solar system in the early 1970s and, once it had done that, was destined to sail off into mysterious, deep space. Just in case another civilization should spot this traveling robot, scientists attached a small gold plate to it explaining in pictures where the robot came from and who sent it. On the plate is a drawing of a man and woman and a star map showing which star is our sun and which planet is ours. A few hundred years from now some extraterrestrial patrolling spaceship may haul in our robot and read the little "hello" attached to it.

A little closer to earth but still in outer space, there are new kinds of space soldiers circling the earth. They are armed robots called hunter-killer satellites which are under instructions to seek out camera-equipped spy satellites and destroy them. So far, only the Russians seem to have these robot killers which were discovered after American space experts began noticing that some of their best spy satellites were mysteriously blinded or just seemed to disappear in outer space.

Some of these hunter-killer satellites are "suicide robots" that move up next to their targets and explode, destroying both the target and themselves. Others are equipped with laser guns that shoot straight into the camera "eyes" of the spy satellites, permanently blinding them. In the future, some experts predict these killers will also be equipped with a special death ray called a proton beam. This never misses its target and can drill through the toughest of materials with ease. It's faster and deadlier than a guided missile and is impossible to stop.

Because of these new space robots, many experts believe that the next big war could be fought not here on earth but in the silent, eerie blackness of space. It would be duels between deadly machines equipped with computer-fast minds and deadly one-shot ray guns. All we humans on earth could do about such battles is watch.

Here on earth, robots are now taking the place of people. At one General Motors factory, specially trained teams of robots work on the assembly lines, welding car bodies together.

They work so fast, they can weld together an entire car in a little more than thirty seconds. At one Army base, robots are now sent out to do the dangerous job of deactivating bombs.

In some office buildings, robot messengers roam the halls, picking up and delivering mail and running errands for humans. These are intelligent little carts that can call their own elevators to go to another floor; that know enough to stop when someone or something is in front of them; and that make their way around corridors by using their robot eyes to follow a white guideline painted on the floor.

Some Russian scientists have even invented a special ocean-exploring robot that looks like a giant mechanical spider. It's equipped with six flexible legs and a special laser beam eye that will let it wander across the deepest and darkest part of the ocean floor without stumbling or falling. It can even compress its mechanical body to squeeze through narrow corridors or other tight spots.

None of these robots is smarter than the humans who made them. In fact, some of the machines are completely "dumb," that is they have to have a human telling them what to do all the time. Others have been taught to do a certain job by a pre-recorded memory that was installed inside them, but all they know is what is in that memory. They can't learn any more on their own. None of these kinds of machines could ever outsmart a person.

There are other machines that come very

close to being quicker and smarter than a human and, if scientists are not careful, may be controlling humans someday. There is one robot, for example, that can instantly memorize the layout of a room and can find its way around in it even in the dark. Another robot can assemble a complicated piece of machinery just by studying a pile of the machine parts scattered in front of it.

Scientists have taught robots to listen to people, to talk, and even to sing. One robot made its stage debut in New York in an opera about a woman scientist who builds an intelligent machine that falls in love with her and eventually tries to kill her. There is another robot that can read sentences out loud which have been typed into its brain. The way it does this is to scan its memory bank for the right pronunciation of a word and then recite the word through its loudspeaker mouth. Finally, experts in what is called artificial intelligence, that is making "smart" machines, have built a robot that can listen to and understand a human speaking to it. The robot makes its replies by means of a typewriter.

One of the strangest of all the robots is probably one designed by Dr. Joseph Weizenbaum of the Massachusetts Institute of Technology. He built a robot psychiatrist named "Doctor" which talks to people by a typewriter connected to its brain. He types out his questions and the people type out their answers. One woman who talked to Doctor said that it cured her of her problems and another person asked to be a regular patient of Doctor!

Other scientists at Stanford University in California even designed a robot brain, called "Parry," which had its own personality. It was so convincing that a group of psychiatrists who "spoke" to Parry and five real humans by teletype machines couldn't tell which was the robot and which was the human.

There are also special robot watchmen used at top-secret government bases which are impossible to trick. No one who is not in the robots' memory bank can get past them. These robots have been taught some unusual ways to identify a human. They can identify a human by making a computer-fast scan of his fingerprints, the length of his fingers, or the way he signs his name.

As smart as many of these robots are, none of them are a match for a smart human. The best human chess player can still beat the best robot chess player, and no machine knows more than the people who built it. That may change, says Dr. Weizenbaum, when scientists build U.I.M., the Ultra-Intelligent Machine. This would be a true Master Machine, one that really could, if we weren't careful, turn us all into robots.

As a robot, U.I.M. could be very dangerous because it could actually learn more all by itself, something no machine can do today. It could build more machines like itself and even teach them how to make themselves smarter than their parent machine. Even equipped with something as simple as television-camera eyes, the U.I.M. would be smart enough to tell what people were thinking just by watching the way they behaved. It could control us directly by brain radios, or indirectly by taking charge of all the computers and robots that *we* now control. Worst of all, there would be no escape from U.I.M., not even in outer space. The U.I.M.'s private army of space robots would methodically hunt down and destroy all disobedient humans trying to leave the planet. It would be a world, maybe even a solar system, controlled by a cold, calculating, invincible robot.

Voodoo Power

Out of breath, out of water, half crazy with fear, the aborigine man stumbled across the wasteland of the Australian desert, baking under the heat of the midday sun. Although weak from exhaustion and days of scrambling in the unbearable heat, the man rarely paused in his panicky flight. When he did stop, it was to search the horizon behind him for a sign of his hunter. No matter how far or how fast he ran, he found he was never out of sight of a distant, lone figure walking relentlessly in his direction.

That solitary person was a Kurdaicha, a voodoo magic killer hired by an aborigine witch doctor to deliver a death curse to his intended victim. Once a Kurdaicha had been selected to deliver a curse, he could not return to his village until his mission was completed. As required by tribal traditions, he wore the bizarre costume of his cult. Instead of clothes, he had kangaroo fur glued to his naked skin with a paste made of dried human blood. Over his face he wore a weird looking mask made entirely of feathers. On his feet were special stalking shoes designed to leave no tracks even in the loose sand of the desert.

The killer carried no weapons except for a specially prepared curse bone in the pouch that hung from his waist. The bone was from the leg of a human skeleton and was sharpened to a point on one end. At the other end was a knob of sticky resin with human hair braided through it. This hex bone had been carefully crafted by a Nangarri, an aborigine witch doctor, to deliver the curse imbedded in it to the victim for whom it was intended.

It would only be a matter of time before the Kurdaicha got close enough to unleash the curse in the bone on its victim. The voodoo-magic killer was a superb hunter and a man of great patience. He would take all the time necessary, weeks, months, or even years, to track down his victim and unleash the hex. There were few places in the Australian wilderness where the man could hide from this grim, determined killer.

The cursed man, who was himself an experienced hunter, managed to elude his Kurdaicha for several weeks by staying on the run night and day. He knew that every moment he paused, death, in the form of that strangely dressed killer, was moving closer. The man used all the tricks he knew to throw the Kurdaicha off his trail, but none of them worked for long. Somehow the killer always managed to pick up the tracks once again and continue his hunt.

One day the man's luck finally ran out. As he stepped into a clearing, he had the uncanny feeling that a pair of eyes was watching him. As he slowly turned around, he saw his killer, the Kurdaicha, crouched under a bush aiming the point of the hex bone straight at him.

The man stood transfixed, staring at the bone. His eyes widened with horror as he realized what was about to happen. Slowly the Kurdaicha began singing the death chant that would unleash the curse. The victim stood there seeing nothing but the sharp tip of the white bone, hearing nothing but the high-pitched whine of the chanting killer.

When the chant was over, the victim felt death pass into him, and the Kurdaicha, seeing that the curse had taken hold, quietly put the bone away and left the man to his fate. At first the man did nothing but stand there, stunned by the curse. Then he slowly collapsed to the ground, his eyes glazed over in terror. For a while he lay still on the ground, feeling the spirit of the pointed curse bone tearing away at his insides. A short time later he began to moan, quietly at first, then louder and louder as he realized that his life was finished.

After a while the man collected his strength and headed back to his village to die. He told no one what had happened, yet his fellow tribesmen knew he was marked for death. Everyone avoided him. Even his wife and children stayed away to avoid being infected by the curse. He returned to his deserted hut and lay there for days, neither eating nor drinking anything. At the end of those days, the man died. The hex bone had done its job.

For years the people who knew better — doctors and other experts — claimed that stories like this were a lot of nonsense. No man would simply lie down and die because a bone had been pointed at him. Most experts thought all those stories about hex bones and death were purely superstition until they started checking into them. What they found surprised them. There were definite forces of voodoo magic at work.

Among the aborigines of Australia, for example, the most powerful and most feared man is the Nangarri, the local witch doctor. His power to make a hex bone and send the Kurdaicha out to deliver the curse inspires awe and terror in his fellow aborigines.

Even today there is little known about the mysterious hex bone other than the fact that it is usually made from the leg bone from the skeleton of a man or baby. The death curse is infused in the bone by a special secret ceremony that only the witch doctor knows. This ritual, the aborigines believe, gives the bone a spirit that is released when a special killing chant is sung. At that moment, a ghostly bone flies straight into the heart of the cursed person and stays there, tearing at the victim until death comes.

Doctors who worked among the aborigines were convinced there was probably a simpler reason. Although many doctors had seen natives die after a hex bone was pointed at them, the medical men were certain that the real cause of these mysterious deaths was poison. Among their many powers and abilities, the witch doctors were skilled in the art of concocting deadly poisons from certain wild plants that grew in the Australian bush. Because of this, doctors believed the real cause of death wasn't the curse but some poison cleverly slipped into the victim's food or drink. But try as they might, the doctors could never find anything suspicious in the victims' bodies.

For example, one day an Australian doctor, Dr. Peter Clarke, saw an aborigine walk into his hospital and claim that a witch doctor had pointed a hex bone at him and, as a result, he would soon die. Dr. Clarke thoroughly examined the man immediately, taking special care to check his blood for traces of poison. Clarke found nothing suspicious. The man was exceptionally strong and healthy and had no signs of any illness.

In spite of that, the man claimed he would soon die and lay down on a hospital bed to wait for death. By sundown of the same day, he had already begun to get weaker and started to lose consciousness. To help him recover from his mysterious ailment, the doctor asked a friend of the aborigine to come by and encourage the man to get better. After the visitor arrived and took one look at his friend lying in the bed, he said, "There is nothing you can do, Doctor. Soon he will die." The next morning the man was found dead in his hospital bed. A thorough medical examination of the body did not uncover any reason for the mysterious death.

As a result of stories such as this, some doctors now believe it is possible that people can die as a result of curses but, as yet, no one knows why these bizarre deaths occur. One theory about curse deaths offered by Dr. Walter Cannon of Harvard Medical School is that the victim who believes in curses literally scares himself to death. Belief in the power of the witch doctor is so strong that when a victim sees a hex bone pointed at him, he simply gives up and dies. Somehow the victim unconsciously manages to slow down his heartbeat and finally stop his own heart completely at the time of death.

It is also possible to use this same power of belief to undo a curse that has been aimed at someone. One Australian doctor had an aborigine come to his hospital claiming he would soon die because a hex bone had been pointed at him. Again, although the man appeared to be perfectly healthy, he grew seriously ill hours after he arrived at the hospital.

This time the doctor decided to get the witch doctor who pointed the bone to cure the man.

The medical doctor told the witch doctor that if the sick man died, the hospital would no longer provide food to the witch doctor or his family and that he and his family would have to move out of the village. After hearing this, the witch doctor went straight to the dying man's bedside and told him there had been some misunderstanding. There was no curse, the witch doctor explained. The hex bone he had pointed at the man wasn't even loaded. The whole thing was just a joke. After hearing this, the sick man sat up, took a few drinks of water, and walked out of the hospital to go back to work.

The aborigines also believe that one witch doctor can sometimes undo the curse of another. The family of a cursed person will often hire a witch doctor to perform elaborate secret ceremonies to remove the ghost of the hex bone that has been fired into a victim's body. The chants and the prayers needed to do this will only work if the Nangarri, or witch doctor, is left alone with the cursed person. After many hours or sometimes many days of ceremonies, a successful witch doctor will finally emerge holding a small piece of pointed bone — the hex bone — in his hands. When the dying victim sees this, a miraculous change comes over him. He usually recovers instantly and shows no trace of his close brush with death.

There are other kinds of black magic that do not depend on the belief of the victim but which can be just as deadly. Some witch doctors seem to be gifted with special psychic powers that help their curses work. In the mountain villages of Tibet, for example, psychic power is responsible for the ritual of self-killing in which a person marked for execution dies by slashing himself to death with a specially cursed knife.

When a group of village elders decides that someone must die for committing a serious wrong, they call in their witch doctor, a Tibetan priest, to curse the knife of execution. The witch doctor takes the knife and goes off by himself to a cave. There he will spend months trying to project certain powers into the knife by reenacting the same scene over and over again in his mind. What he sees is the victim picking up the knife and plunging it into his own chest. In this way, the witch doctor, or Tibetan priest, believes he will eventually infuse in the knife a power all its own to kill the man who touches it.

Once the Tibetan priest feels the knife has absorbed enough power, he then hides it in the home of the victim. The Tibetans believe that when the condemned man finds the knife and actually touches it, the cursing powers of the knife are activated. The cursed man will then find his hand uncontrollably driving the knife into his chest over and over again.

Skeptical outsiders who have investigated this self-killing ritual have found that even in Tibet today there are many bloody cases of self-killings with cursed knives. The real power of the curse, according to investigators, is not from the cursed knife itself but from a kind of long range hypnosis that occurs while the priest is preparing the knife. The Tibetan witch doctor has psychic powers that help him project to the victim the picture of the victim stabbing himself to death. In this way, the priest eventually hypnotizes the victim so that when he sees the knife, his first impulse is to drive it into his chest.

Black magic is not restricted to the remote areas of the world like the Australian desert or the mountains of Tibet. It is practiced in parts of the United States today in the form known as voodoo and has been since slaves first brought this strange belief to this country in the seventeenth century. Some of the people that had been captured in the African country that is now called Dahomey belonged to a cult that worshipped the snake god, Vodu. Many of these Vodu worshippers ended up in Haiti where Vodu, or Voodoo as it is now called, is still widely practiced. Others ended up working on the tobacco and cotton plantations in the American South. Some of them kept the tradition of Voodoo alive and passed on the secret ceremonies and rituals connected with it.

Voodoo still exists in some parts of the South and in the larger cities of the North as well, although it has changed somewhat over the centuries, borrowing some of its symbols and ceremonies from other sources. One part of the cult that has remained unchanged, however, is that only certain people, called voodoo kings or queens, are considered to have the magical powers to cure or curse people. Often there are times when these people are called upon to use their powers for a special kind of voodoo justice.

In one famous case in New Orleans back in the 1930s, a girl was murdered by her boyfriend in a lovers' quarrel. They were standing by one of the canals that run through the city when, in the course of the argument, the boy hit the girl, knocking her into the water. He then ran off leaving her to drown. A night watchman who heard the commotion arrived too late to save the girl but saw her murderer.

In the days that followed, the police searched the city for the girl's killer but were unable to find a clue as to where he might be. Finally, the family of the murdered girl decided to search him out and get their revenge their own way. They consulted a voodoo queen on what had to be done to get even. According to the queen's instructions, the family prepared the girl's body for a curse burial. They placed a fresh egg in each hand of the corpse, tied the wrists together with a rope, and lay her body face down in the coffin. Then for two days and nights they kept a special vigil by the body saying voodoo prayers to make the curse work. On the third day, they buried the girl and waited.

The day after the burial, the boyfriend showed up. His body was found floating face down in the canal right near the spot where the girl had been murdered. The police claimed the man had killed himself in his sorrow over murdering his girlfriend. But the family of the murdered girl thought differently.

Other kinds of voodoo curses can take years to work as one University of Pennsylvania psychologist, Dr. Martin Seligman, found out in a 22-year-long case. The story began in a small Georgia town where on one Friday the thirteenth three girl babies were born to three mothers. The midwife who delivered the children claimed that being born on that day was a bad omen and each of the girls would live very short lives. One girl, the woman predicted, would never live to see her sixteenth birthday. The second, she said, would never live past the age of 21. The third girl would be dead before she was 23.

The first girl, in fact, died in a car accident when she was 15 years old. The second was in a nightclub the night before her twenty-second birthday and was killed by a stray bullet fired during a gunfight in the club. That left the third girl who looked to her approaching twenty-third birthday with increasing terror.

Two days before that birthday, the girl finally decided to get help. She went to a hospital and, insane with fear, begged the doctors to let her stay there and protect her from this death curse. Although the woman seemed perfectly healthy, the doctors thought it might help calm her down if they let her rest for a few days. The next morning, the morning before the birthday, a nurse found the woman dead in her hospital bed. Totally mystified, the doctors examined the woman's body but were unable to find any reason for her sudden death.

According to Dr. Seligman, who investigated the case, the woman had died because she believed so strongly in the power of the old witch's prediction. She reacted to the story of coming death the same way the aborigine reacted to having a hex bone pointed at him. In some mysterious, unconscious way, the woman's terror became a deadly force that destroyed her life before her twenty-third birthday, just as the old woman had predicted.

In addition to all this black magic, there are the healing powers of white magic. One of the best examples of this is the medicine man of the Navajo Indians. While the Indians have adopted many of the modern conveniences of the white man, they still follow the tradition of going to their local medicine man who treats their problems and ailments with age-old cures and ceremonies passed on from father to son over the centuries. In many cases, the Indians find their own doctors are better at curing certain ills than conventional doctors with all their pills and needles.

Navajo medicine men have different skills, each of which plays a part in their tradition of healing. For example, there is one group of medicine men that tries to find the cause of ailments. The Navajos believe that there are twelve Indian gods who can offer advice in these matters and that only certain people can talk to these gods. Medicine men believe that very often someone falls ill if he either has been cursed, or if he, or someone in his family, has committed some offense against nature — needlessly killing or injuring an animal for example. In such cases, the gods tell the medicine man the cause of the sickness.

There is another group of medicine men who "read" the stars for clues to find the cause of sickness. Usually the answer comes from a particular star that in some mysterious way shows what part of the body is ailing and what kind of medicine it needs.

There is another group of medicine men, the hand tremblers, who pray to the gods for information about a sick person. If they make contact, after a while one of their arms will begin shaking and flopping around as a sign that one of the gods is trying to talk through them. When this happens, the medicine man goes into a trance and begins speaking in a strange language. Once the trance is over, he tells the sick person what his problem is and what has to be done to cure it.

For the cure, a person may then contact one of the tribe's herbalists. These are Navajos who know which desert plants are safe to use as medicines and which special prayers must be said to get them to work properly. Knowledge about these plants has been passed down through generations of medicine men for centuries. In fact, many of the medicines made from these plants that had been used by the Indians long before the white man set foot in

America have only recently been rediscovered by modern medicine.

Sometimes it happens that the herbalists can't help, and more drastic steps must be taken. In those cases, the sick person may then contact the most highly skilled of all medicine men, the healer. These men have been trained for their work since childhood and have the skills of not only the herbalists and medicine men who find disease causes, but they must know other things besides. They must know all the secret prayers and charts of the medicine men, some of which take days to recite, and they must know all the myths and stories of the tribe's religion and be able to repeat them word for word from memory. In addition, they have to know the complicated ritual of the tribal dances; they must learn the delicate art of sand painting, that is, using natural colors to draw important ceremonial images on the desert floor; and finally they have to learn which treatments are appropriate for which diseases. They have chants and ceremonies for almost every ailment — from an ordinary toothache to total blindness. Each one is different and each must be recited or sung a certain way to be completely effective.

These healers have many of the skills and some of the knowledge of the white man's doctors and, in some instances, have shown themselves to be better than the white man's doctor. On one occasion, a Navajo patient with a sharp pain in his side went to a white doctor who worked on the reservation. After examining him, the doctor said there was probably something wrong with the man's kidneys. The local healer disagreed, saying the problem was the man's appendix. When the white doctor operated on the patient to settle the matter once and for all, he found the man's kidneys were fine but the man's appendix was infected and ready to burst.

In another more mysterious case, a young boy seemed to be constantly suffering from colds all year, and none of the medicines the white doctors gave him seemed to help. Finally, the family took the boy to a medicine man to find out the real cause of his illness. After praying to the Navajo gods, the medicine man said he was told that someone in the boy's family had injured a porcupine and, as punishment, the boy had to suffer from his colds. As proof that the insulted animal was a porcupine, the medicine man put his mouth on the boy's neck and, in front of the astonished parents, drew out a long, thin porcupine needle with his lips.

The spirit of the animal had to be appeased, the medicine man said. To do this the family had to carve the figure of a porcupine out of wood and leave it under a "friendly" tree which the medicine man selected for them. The parents did as they were told and from that day on, the boy's mysterious colds disappeared completely.

Many doctors have been so impressed by the ability of the medicine men to cure people with their special ancient chants and ceremonies that they've invited the healers to work in hospitals with them treating Indians. In some cases the healers are learning the medical techniques of the white man so that they are equally able to handle drugs and diagnoses as well as to perform the ancient rituals. In no instance, however, has a white man ever been allowed to learn the secrets of the healers. Like all special skills and powers, like the powers of the Nangarri of the aborigines and the voodoo kings and queens, these powers and skills are still reserved for the chosen few who understand their secrets.

The Many Moods of Your Body

Even though he had slept well the night before, Captain Richard Brock still felt a little strange, a little tired. As the pilot of flight 514, this bothered him since he always tried to be in the best possible shape. Fortunately, the sky was clear and bright on that December day in 1974 and, although the landing approach to Dulles Airport just outside of Washington, D.C. was a little tricky, he had made the landing many times before and didn't anticipate any serious trouble. He knew that even feeling as tired as he did, both he and his co-pilot, Leonard Kreschek, could handle just about any landing problem that came up.

What Captain Brock didn't know was that Leonard Kreschek was also feeling a little groggy that day. For some reason he had trouble concentrating and as a result, he was constantly double-checking as he performed his co-pilot duties, to make sure he was doing everything he should. Right now he was preparing for the last important maneuver before landing at Dulles. To get to the runway, the plane first had to climb up over a mountain range and then dive down the other side to make its landing. Getting this part of the approach right was a matter of life and death.

Meanwhile at the airport, flight controller Merle Dameron concentrated his attention on flight 514 which appeared as a moving dot of light on his radar screen. This was just part of a day's work for Dameron who had been guiding planes in for twenty years. He knew the approach patterns to Dulles Airport as well as he knew his own name and address. In addition, he had a kind of sixth sense about when a plane was in trouble just by glancing at his radar screen. For some reason, however, that sixth sense didn't seem to be working today. He had trouble focusing his attention on his work. He felt odd, not really sick, but not healthy and alert either.

Suddenly Dameron sat bolt upright and stared at the radar screen. Something was terribly wrong with the route flight 514 was taking. At first he wasn't sure what the problem was but then, in an instant he realized what was about to happen. The airplane had failed to start its climb and at its present altitude was due to collide with a mountain any second. Just as Dameron clicked on his radio to tell the pilot to pull up, he noticed that the small dot of light that had been flight 514 disappeared from the radar screen. At that instant the airplane with 92 people aboard had slammed into a wall of stone and had become a huge fireball of flaming metal, rolling down the side of the mountain. No one survived the crash.

The one question that mystified all the investigators who studied the crash was: Why did it happen? Both the pilot and co-pilot were experienced men who had made the flight many times before. The flight controller had guided thousands of planes over the same flight path without any accidents. The plane itself was in good working order. There were no malfunctions that anyone could find in a close examination of the wreckage. In short, there was no good reason why the plane should have collided with the side of the mountain.

There are some people who believe the crash had nothing to do with the abilities of the people involved or any kind of mechanical failure. The real cause of the crash could have been an unfortunate timing of three clocks. These were not the kind of clocks most people use to tell time, but mysterious, natural timepieces that to a certain extent control people's moods and health with steady up and down changes. These changes are called biorhythms and, according to the experts who study them, they are often responsible for those days when for no apparent reason you feel tired, depressed, or have trouble concentrating. Biorhythms can also produce days when you feel as though everything is going all right, or, most dangerous, days when you feel a little unsettled and confused.

According to biorhythm experts, the "up" days are called plus days, the "down" days are called minus days, and the days of confusion are called zero days. According to biorhythm expert, Bernard Gittelson, each of the three people involved in the crash — the pilot, the co-pilot, and the flight controller — were all suffering from minus biorhythm days or the more dangerous zero days without realizing it. As a result each man may have been feeling a little more tired, or a little less attentive than usual. Because of this, the pilot may have misread the instrument giving him the altitude, and his co-pilot may not have noticed the mistake. At the airport, the ground controller's discovery that the aircraft was in danger, and his attempt to warn the pilot, may have been clouded by the fact that his biorhythms were interfering with his thinking and his reactions. The combination of these slip-ups, Gittelson says, could have caused the air disaster that finally happened.

These mysterious biorhythms were not unique to the pilot, the co-pilot, and the ground controller. All of us have biorhythms ticking away inside us from the day we are born to the day we die. They are just one of many kinds of clocks that seem to be at work inside the body. Probably the most familiar body clock is the one that controls when we wake up and when we sleep. Although most people once thought the reason we awoke and slept was the rising and setting of the sun, one adventurous group of scientists showed that something inside the body is in charge. The group spent weeks in the dark depths of a large cave, never once seeing a sunrise or sunset. In spite of that, their body clocks made them drowsy and woke them up over a 24-hour period just as though the sun were shining in the cave.

More mysterious are other kinds of cycles that seem to affect the health of the body. For example, doctors know that the same dose of medicine may have a weak or powerful effect on a sick person, depending on what time of the day a person receives it. There are even cases of people who have strange ailments that come and go with an odd regularity. In one instance, a star soccer player on an English team had a bad knee that would swell up with such regularity, the team scheduled their big games on the days when they knew their star's knee would not be bothering him.

Biorhythms work with the same kind of regularity and they influence how sad or happy you feel, how tired or energetic you are, and even how well you learn. According to the biorhythm theory, there is a natural clock that controls our bodies, our emotions, and our minds according to three different cycles. Each cycle has two parts: an "up" phase when everything is going well, and a "down" phase when the cycle is slowly winding down. Each cycle takes a different amount of time to run its course. The physical cycle that controls the body is 23 days long. The cycle of the emotions takes 28 days, and the intellectual one for the mind takes 33 days. They all start the day we are born and can be drawn on a special chart showing the ups and downs. For example, if someone is born on the first day of May, a month which is 31 days long, his biorhythm ups and downs for the first month of his life would look like the following drawing:

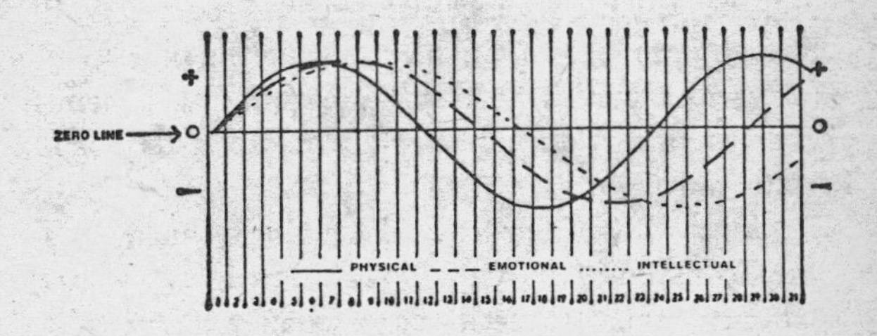

Drawn this way, each of the cycles looks like an "S" lying on its side showing each cycle equally divided into good and bad days above and below a zero line. This means that during the first 11½ days of the 23-day physical cycle, the part of the cycle above the zero line, a person should feel strong and energetic and do well in sports and other kinds of physical activities. As a person's biorhythms cross the zero line into the second 11½ days, he should start to feel a little more tired, slower in his reactions, and maybe even feel sick. Something similar happens during the 28-day long emotional cycle. For the first 14 days, a person will usually feel very cheerful and peppy but as he gets into the second 14 days his mood will be more and more serious and the person may also get a little depressed. In the 33-day intellectual cycle, a person will usually feel bright and alert during the first 16½ days, but may have trouble learning or remembering things during the "down" 16½-day second half.

Every day of our lives, these biorhythm waves are constantly moving up or down, taking us through these three kinds of changes. Our best days will occur when the waves are at their peak. The worst days happen when the waves have sunk to their lowest point. Biorhythm experts also claim that the most dangerous day, as far as our health is concerned, is the crossover day when one or more biorhythm wave crosses the zero line. During this time, a person is neither in an up nor a down biorhythm phase. Instead, the body is completely off balance, and any unusual problem, especially sickness or crisis, could have deadly consequences. For example, the day that flight 514 crashed, the flight controller was going through a critical day, as the crossover day is called, in his physical biorhythm cycle. This could very well be the reason why the flight controller didn't immediately realize the airplane was not in the right flight pattern. This critical day, in combination with a low mental biorhythm, may have clouded his mind enough to create that situation.

For centuries, no one suspected there were such complicated three-part changes going on in the body until a German doctor named Wilhelm Fleiss began wondering why some perfectly healthy children became sick when exposed to a disease while others, who seemed to be just as healthy, did not. After a while he noticed that the children seemed to have sick days and healthy days that came and went in regular 23-day cycles.

Just about the same time, in the early 1900s, an Austrian, Dr. Hermann Swoboda, found he could even predict when some of his weaker patients would suffer heart attacks or asthma attacks because their ailments seemed to come in steady 23-day cycles. He also discovered his patients went through predictable up and down changes in their moods every 28 days. Swoboda also made one more discovery. Halfway through every cycle, when a person's biorhythm crossed the zero line, something very peculiar happened. On this critical day, as Swoboda called it, people seemed to have more accidents, they got sick more often, and more people died. A zero day was even more critical if more than one biorhythm crossed the zero line at the same time. When this happened, a person was even more likely than usual to have a disastrous accident or become deathly ill.

While these discoveries were being made, an Austrian teacher named Alfred Teltscher got curious about the fact that even the best of his students seemed to have both good and bad days. After keeping special track of his students' grades and, after checking those of other classes, he noticed that how smart his students were seemed to follow a general pattern. Every 33 days, they would first do very well in class and later do a little less well, flunking a few tests or getting low grades. This 33-day intellectual cycle happened to everyone regardless of how intelligent they were.

For many years scientists have had clues that certain changes in a person's body and mind come and go with a certain regularity. One of the most bizarre examples of this was the case of Mary Lamb, the sister of Charles Lamb, a famous nineteenth-century English writer. Mary had unpredictable spells of insanity that would disappear as suddenly as they appeared. When she was normal, Mary was a quiet, pleasant woman who was devoted to her parents. During one of her insane spells, however, she completely lost control of herself, killed her sick mother and then tried to kill her father as well. Because of her brother's influence, she was saved from execution and allowed to stay with him. While in her brother's care, Mary continued to have fits of madness. Fortunately, her brother was able to spot these fits developing before they got too dangerous. When they began, he would quietly put on Mary's straitjacket and lead her down the road to a nearby asylum where she stayed until the madness passed.

Because of many such cases, some experts began to wonder if there were any connection between biorhythms and the onset of insanity. Doctors in one New York State mental hospital noticed their patients seemed to have sane days and insane days with some regularity. To find out if there really were some patterns of insanity, the doctors kept careful track of when their patients seemed normal and when they were insane. They discovered there seemed to be a new cycle of sane and insane behavior that would start up every 28 days, the same length of time as the biorhythm for the emotions.

A Swiss scientist named Hans Schwing made another intriguing discovery when he decided to investigate the cause of some car accidents. He had heard of the biorhythm theory and wanted to see if there were any connection between biorhythms and accidents. Schwing got the birthdates of 700 people who had been in accidents and, in each case, figured out their biorhythm charts on the day of the accident. He found that in well over half the cases, the accident happened on a person's critical day, when one or more of his biorhythm curves were crossing over the zero line. Based on this discovery, Schwing said a person is five times more likely to have an accident on a critical day than on any other day.

The more biorhythms cross the zero line on the same day, the more dangerous that day is according to the biorhythm experts. On the average, there are about seven days in the year when two biorhythms cross the zero line on the same day. These double zero days, as they are called, are especially dangerous if the two biorhythms involved are the physical and emotional ones. Even more rare and more dangerous are triple zero days when all three biorhythms cross at once. This will happen perhaps one time a year.

One deadly example of what the triple zero days can do is the case of Benny "Kid" Paret, a top-ranked welterweight boxer. In 1963, he was matched against fighter Emile Griffith, in what promised to be an exciting bout for the welterweight title. Neither Paret nor Griffith liked each other, and neither made much secret of that fact. This mutual dislike promised to add a particularly interesting element to the fight. Both men were at the peak of condition, and both were considered to be an equal match for each other. For these reasons, boxing fans expected to see an exciting bout. The match was scheduled for March 24, a day which, unknown to anyone, happened to be a rare, triple-zero day for Benny Paret.

The night of the big fight, the fans were a little disappointed in Paret's performance. He seemed a little slower than usual and just wasn't punching as hard as he usually did. Emile Griffith took full advantage of this. During round after round, he pounded Paret savagely. During round after round, Paret stumbled out into the ring only to be beaten back into the ropes where he helplessly tried to avoid Griffith's savage attack. Finally, Paret's body just couldn't take any more. After receiving one last punch, he toppled to the canvas and lay there completely unconscious. Griffith was declared the winner by a knockout.

Benny Paret never regained consciousness that night or any night after. After attempts to wake him up failed, he was rushed to the hospital where he stayed in a deep coma for 12 days. The savage beating he took on his triple-zero day had practically destroyed his brain. Unfortunately for him, that twelfth day in the hospital was another critical day, a double-zero day on which two biorhythms crossed. And it was on that day that he died.

Some experts say this could have been avoided if Benny Paret knew the fight was going to take place on his triple-zero day. His triple-zero biorhythms not only interfered with his boxing ability but weakened him physically as well. As a result, he wasn't able to fight in top form and couldn't survive the beating he took.

In the case of other athletes, biorhythms have brought slightly better luck. On the days when swimmer Mark Spitz won his record-breaking string of seven gold medals in the 1972 Olympics, both his physical and emotional biorhythms were at their peaks in the plus cycle, the most ideal of biorhythm situations. Even more remarkable was the way two football fans and biorhythm experts used biorhythms to predict the victories and losses of the Los Angeles Rams during their 1972 season.

Using a specially devised system of team biorhythms, Nancy Lee Roberts and Michael R. Wallerstein figured out the Rams' biorhythms for a specific game and matched them against the biorhythms of their opposing team. To test their method, they matched up team biorhythms for ten games in the coming season and predicted the winners on the basis of who had the more positive, or stronger-looking body rhythms. These predictions were then put in a sealed envelope to be opened at the end of the season. Their season predictions turned out to be correct for nine out of the ten games.

As a grand windup to that year's football season, the two experts charted the biorhythms of the Washington Redskins and the Miami Dolphins, the teams playing in the 1972 Superbowl, and attempted to predict the winner. Although both the experts were Miami Dolphins fans, their results indicated the Redskins would probably be the winners. And they were.

Biorhythms are now taken pretty seriously and are used for things other than predicting the outcome of football games. Since many people seem to have more accidents on zero days or critical days, some companies have started to keep track of the biorhythms of the people who work for them. At United Airlines, here in the United States, computers keep track of employees' biorhythms. When someone is about to have a dangerous zero day, the computer makes a note of it, and that person is warned to be extra careful on those danger days. On Swissair, the national airline of Switzerland, every pilot's biorhythm is closely watched so that two pilots with critical biorhythms will not be flying the same airplane. And in Japan, one bus company keeps track of the biorhythms of its 500 drivers. On a bad day, a driver is warned to be careful before setting out for a day of driving. In every case, knowing about bad days helps keep a lot of people from having accidents. The accident rate dropped drastically after both United Airlines and the Japanese bus company began warning their employees. Swissair has had *no* accidents on flights with biorhythm-matched pilots.

Although all these big companies used computers to figure out the biorhythms, you can do the same thing for your own biorhythms without any fancy computers. All you need is a pencil, paper, and the ability to add and divide.

The way to chart your biorhythms is fairly simple. What you will have to do is add up all the days of your life, from the day you were born up to and including the present. Then divide this total number by the three biorhythm numbers—23, for the physical cycle, 28 for the emotional cycle, and 33 for the mental, or intellectual, cycle — to see where your biorhythm now stands.

Let's suppose, for example, that a girl born on August 8, 1962 wants to figure out her biorhythm and that today is May 3, 1977. Her first step is to add up all the days of her life right up to the present. Since she has not yet reached her fifteenth birthday, she of course is still considered to be 14 years old. The figures for her biorhythm would look like this:

14 years × 365 days	5110
Extra days for leap years which come every four years. (1964, 1968, 1972, and 1976 are leap years.)	4
Number of days from August 8, 1976 up to, and including May 3, 1977.	+ 268
Total number of days in life so far	5382

The next step is to divide by the biorhythm

cycle numbers — 23 for the physical cycle, 28 for the emotional, and 33 for the mental — to find out exactly where she is in each biorhythm cycle. When she does this, she gets these results:

For the physical cycle: 5382 ÷ 23 = 234 completed cycles and 0 days left over.

For the emotional cycle: 5382 ÷ 28 = 192 completed cycles with 6 days left over.

For the mental cycle: 5382 ÷ 33 = 163 complete cycles with 3 days left over.

These numbers tell the girl where her biorhythms stand on May 3, 1977. According to the figures for her physical cycle, she has finished 234 cycles, is now going through a critical zero day, and is also starting a new cycle. Since all cycles start by going "up" first, the next 11½ days will be positive physical days, good for exercising and playing sports. According to her emotional reading, she has finished 192 cycles in her life and is already six days into the 14-day "up" half of the emotional cycle. This means for the next eight days she should feel pretty happy unless something drastic happens to change her mood. Around May 11, her mood should start changing and she might be feeling a little low.

Finally, her intellectual measurement shows that she has already gone three days into the 16½-day positive cycle and so for the next 13½ days she should do pretty well in school and in her homework. After May 17, however, she might have trouble concentrating and may not do as well on tests as she hoped she would.

You can compute your own biorhythms just by following the simple formula used for the 14-year-old girl. The first step is to find out how many days you have lived. To do that add the following:

1. Your age × 365
2. The number of leap years since you were born.
3. The number of days from your last birthday up to and including the present day.

The sum of all these numbers will be the total number of days you've been alive.

The next step is to take this sum and divide it as follows:

Sum ÷ 23 = physical biorhythm

Sum ÷ 28 = emotional biorhythm

Sum ÷ 33 = intellectual biorhythm

After you do your division, you may or may not have some remainder numbers. As in the case of the girl we mentioned before, these will tell you where you stand in each of your three cycles. If the number left over is less than 11½, you are in the positive half of your physical cycle; if it's less than 14, you're in the positive half of your emotional cycle; and if it's less than 16½, you are in the positive half of your intellectual cycle. If the number is larger than any of these, then you are in the negative, or "down" part of the cycle and you may feel tired, a little sad, or just have trouble concentrating as a result. Finally if the number left over is zero, that is if there are in fact no extra numbers, be extra careful because this is a critical, zero-line day.

Now it may be that drawing out your biorhythms may not work if you are one of those rare people who have uneven biorhythms. Experts do believe that this system works for most people and the odds are it should work for you. In fact, most people could really benefit from tracking their biorhythms. Leaders of government might want to wait until their mental cycles are in high gear before they make important decisions. Students might wait until the same mental high waves come along before they tackle a big class project. Athletes could plan more intensive training on their good physical days and take it easy on their low days. Even doctors might adopt the biorhythm system to decide on the best days for operating on their patients.

With all the proof we now have about how well biorhythms work, there is still one mystery left to solve: that is, what controls these steady rhythms. Some believe they are the result of powerful chemicals being periodically pumped into our blood vessels. Others believe changes in the brain's electricity are the reason and still others think the phases of the moon might be responsible for some of them. After years of trying to find the reason, one expert recently threw up his hands in total frustration and admitted, "We just don't have an explanation for these things."

The Third Eye

Mary sat at the table quietly sorting out the colored slips of paper in front of her. As she picked up each piece, she'd brush it lightly with her fingertips and put it in a pile with others of the same color. The scientists standing around her then gave her a large pile of different colored pieces of cloth and she did the same thing with them, announcing what color she had in her hand before she put it in the correct pile.

Although this was something any four-year-old child could do, the experts watching Mary were amazed. She was no child but a fully grown woman with a handicap — she was totally blind and had been since she was five years old. In spite of that fact, she was able to "see" the colored paper and cloth she picked up in a very special way. She was able to "see" with her fingertips. She had a very special gift called dermavision (from the Latin *dermis*, for skin). In some inexplicable way she was actually able to see colors through her skin, not her eyes.

Mary discovered her gift after hearing stories of people who could distinguish different colors by touch, could touch a photograph and tell what was in it and, in some cases, could even read a printed page in a book by touch. She remembered what it was like to see as a little girl and had always hoped that somehow she might be able to see again. Thinking it just might be possible to see with dermavision, Mary went to talk to Dr. Thelma Moss, a world famous expert in extrasensory abilities.

For two months, Mary and Dr. Moss struggled to find the secret of dermavision, starting with very simple experiments using the colors black and white. No matter how hard Mary concentrated, she couldn't find any trace of a talent for seeing with her fingers. Then one day she finally discovered it. She was talking to someone while absent-mindedly touching a piece of black paper when suddenly she noticed it felt warm and rough. She picked up another piece of paper that felt cool and smooth and knew it was white. With a little practice, she was able to tell black from white with just a quick touch. In time, she also learned how red felt to her fingers and eventually reached a point where she could pick out a total of six colors by touch alone.

Eventually her color sensitivity became so strong she could even tell what color someone else was touching simply by tuning her mind to his. Although her sense of color touch finally did develop to an amazing degree, Mary was never able to achieve her dream of being able to read the printed page of a book with her fingertips alone.

As it turns out, Mary's special gift of vision is just one of many strange ways people all over the world have developed sight without using their eyes. In fact, just about everyone has some kind of a third eye, that is, a unique ability to see in a totally different way than we do with our eyes.

One of the most common examples is something called shadow vision. This is a kind of natural radar we have that can warn us when there is a large obstacle in front of us. Many of us have this ability but, because most of us can also see, we usually don't have a reason to use it. Blind people, however, are taught to be aware of this skill and how to use it.

There is a simple test you can take to find out if you are one of the people with the gift of shadow vision. Just close your eyes and walk *very slowly* towards a wall or a closed door. (The shadow vision will not work if you walk too fast). As you get closer to the wall or door, you should be able to sense some kind of faint pressure on the front of your face usually concentrated on your forehead. The pressure will get stronger as you get closer to the obstacle and finally, when you feel it is the strongest, stop and open your eyes. Your face should be about four to six inches away from the wall. Of course, if you don't have this kind of shadow vision, you will walk straight into whatever is in front of you which is another good reason for walking slowly.

This sense was first discovered by individuals who worked with the blind and noticed that some blind people seemed to be able to get around better than others because of this special sense. Even after years of studying this strange, built-in human radar, investigators still don't know exactly how this works or why only some people seem to have it. The only explanation they offer is that this is just one of the many different ways man has of "seeing" without his eyes.

Even more rare than this is the ability to see by touch. Although the woman named Mary did have some of this ability, her talent wasn't nearly as developed as that of Rosa Kuleshova, a simple Russian peasant woman who was probably the person most gifted with this ability. Rosa lived with her family in a mountainous area of the Soviet Union and spent much of her time working with the blind because several members of her own family were blind.

Although she could see, Rosa herself was an expert in reading Braille with her fingertips and always hoped to discover some miracle method of helping the blind to see again. In fact, according to two psychic experts, Sheila Ostrander and Lynn Schroeder, Rosa once had a dream in which she helped the blind to see everything through their fingertips. Then one day the dream came true, at least for her. One day while sitting alone in her room, she picked up an ordinary book and, on an impulse, closed her eyes and laid her hand on an open page.

To her surprise, she found she could actually feel the individual letters printed on the page. With a little more practice she was able to read whole words, sentences, and entire pages in the book by touch alone. After a little more experimentation, she found she could also see different colors the same way and could even describe the contents of a photograph just by touching it.

Both excited and confused about her newly discovered ability, Rosa decided to go to her local doctor in the hope he could explain just how it was she could see by touch. At first the doctor was convinced Rosa's imagination had run away from her and refused to take her claims seriously; but after she insisted that he see her, he decided to give her a test to silence her once and for all.

After blindfolding Rosa, the doctor asked her to identify the color of each slip of paper he handed her and, later, to read by touch sentences from newspapers and magazines he had around the office. Rosa passed both tests with flying colors and the doctor was convinced.

In time, her reputation spread to Moscow where some of the best psychic experts in Russia invited Rosa to come and display her talents. Even the most skeptical of these experts were convinced by her dazzling display of fingertip vision while her eyes were covered. They blindfolded her and held their hands over her eyes as they tested her, but nothing seemed to affect her ability to read and see with her hands almost as well as with her eyes. Her hands were so sensitive, she could read the page of a book or identify a piece of colored cloth covered with glass. She could even tell what color light was being shone on her hand. The scientists were ecstatic.

Even more people heard about Rosa, and before long she had become a big celebrity in Moscow. She began performing in theaters to sold-out houses, and she was famous throughout the country. Unfortunately, Rosa's fame began to go to her head and before long she began making claims that she was able to perform feats that were impossible even for her. She said, for example, that she could read a page of print covered by a tall pile of books just by touching the top of the pile. She had to cheat to perform tricks like this and finally one night she was caught.

The shame was more than she could stand. Rosa went crazy and had to be confined in a mental hospital. Just as mysteriously as they appeared, her marvelous gifts disappeared, and Rosa, the star of psychics in Russia, became a broken and disgraced woman.

Scientists both here and in Russia who had the opportunity to study Rosa were convinced that her talents were genuine and that it was possible for some people to learn them. Among the things that have been learned about dermavision is that children are better at learning it than adults; that even though a person may be blind or blindfolded, someone using dermavision still needs plenty of light to see with his fingertips; and finally, people who have suffered some kind of damage to their brain's vision center cannot learn dermavision.

People who have this skill or learn it report they can guess colors because each has a certain temperature to the touch. Red, for example, always feels hot. Yellow and orange are warm to the touch, and shades of blue and violet are cool. Also red, green, and dark blue usually feel a little rough and sticky, while light blue and yellow feel slippery. Orange and violet, on the other hand, are not sticky but feel rough to sensitive fingers.

You can find out for yourself if you have a special sense of touch with a few simple tests. Ask a friend to pick out a number of slips of paper all the same size and all cut from the same type of paper and keep them hidden from you. Put on a blindfold and have your friend hand you the slips. To make things easy on yourself, first start with two colors such as red and light blue. Using only your sense of touch, separate what you think are the reds from the blues, and when all the slips of paper have been separated, take off your blindfold and see how well you've done. Don't be discouraged if you don't get it at first; try to be as relaxed as possible, and try to follow your instincts in choosing colors. You may just confuse yourself if you think too much about your choice.

Even if you find you don't have any special gift for seeing by touch, you may be one of those people who can see color with another sense, such as hearing. The gift of "seeing" with your ears is called synesthesia. Someone with this gift sees a certain color in his mind's eye when he hears a certain sound. That noise could be anything from a musical note to a clap of thunder, and the ability to turn it into a color is not something that can be learned or taught. It just seems to happen to some people.

One of the most famous people who was synesthesic was a classical music composer named Alexander Scriabin. He literally could not play music without seeing colors flowing through his mind. The influence of these colors was so strong that eventually he even wrote a special piece of music to be played on a strange instrument called a color organ. For every note it would play, a different colored light would go on. By using this instrument, Scriabin could let everyone see the music as he saw it as well as listen to it.

Some synesthesia experts claim that everyone is born with this special gift, but only a few people take the time to develop or enjoy it. For the people who do use the gift, music is their richest source of colors.The amazing thing about synesthesia is that the same sound may look different to different people, so what might be a blue musical note to some people will look like a green note to others.

Everyone with synesthesia does agree that the loudness or softness of a note and the musical instrument playing it can change the colors. Loud music looks brighter to most people, while the colors conjured up by quieter music is softer and dimmer. Also, high-pitched instruments such as violins and flutes seemed to remind some people of definite shapes and colors. When gifted people hear these instruments, they claim they see red or yellow squares, rectangles, triangles, and circles dancing through their minds. Low-pitched instruments such as tubas and cellos create mind pictures of blobs and swirls of dark colors such as brown or deep, dark blues. To a person with a strong sense of synesthesia, an entire orchestra playing could be visualized as a whole cartoon show of colored shapes dancing through the listener's mind.

Ordinary words can have a colorful effect as one British scientist, Sir Francis Galton, discovered. In studying synesthesia, Sir Francis found, for example, that the days of the week could look different to some people. For example, one person told him that Tuesday looked like a pale gray blob, Wednesday was a greenish-yellow oval, Thursday was a reddish brown square, and Friday was a large yellow smudge.

Sir Francis found that even basic sounds such as the five vowels — A, E, I, O, and U — have distinctive colors. The most common that was used to describe A was red; for E and I it was white; for O it was black; and for U it was dark green or brown. One French poet even composed a poem to the different vowels describing A as black; E as white; I, red; O, blue; and U as green. Although this was a slightly different version of the more commonly seen vowel colors, the fact that it was written over 100 years ago shows that people have long been aware of this gift.

You might want to test someone you know for synesthesia simply by asking them if they think of any colors when they hear the five vowels. If they do, ask what colors they see in their mind. For the sake of comparison you might want to ask a number of people and see which colors seem to be the most popular. If the experts are right, you might uncover a few people with a hidden talent for synesthesia.

It is also possible you may discover an even stranger talent connected with synesthesia. For reasons that no one can explain, there are some people who not only see a certain color when they hear a sound, they actually taste a certain kind of food as well. According to synesthesia expert Dr. Lawrence Marks, one woman claimed that every time she heard the name "Francis," she could actually taste baked beans. In addition, she claimed the word "Italy" tasted like pickled onions to her. In another case, a man said that a certain high-pitched note left the taste of a garlic pickle on his tongue! Obviously such taste-sensitive people have to be careful of the music they listen to — especially if they are on diets!

You may not have any signs of any of these gifts of synesthesia or dermavision, but one thing you and every other human being does have is an actual third eye buried inside your skull. It's a small lump of tissue, about the size of a walnut, attached to the front part of your brain. It's called the pineal gland, but it could just as well be called the mystery gland since brain experts still aren't sure exactly what it does. All they know about it is that it produces powerful chemicals that control a lot of what goes on inside our bodies. It has something to do with everything from getting sleepy and hungry to how fast we grow. There are also some who believe that at one time in man's past it may also have been a kind of third eye and, in certain ways, may still be.

One reason for this is that even today there are some animals whose pineal glands are not buried deep inside their heads as ours are, but instead, the gland pokes right through the forehead. For example, there are some kinds of lizards whose pineal gland looks like a large white eye growing out of the top of their heads. It has its own lens just as regular eyes do and seems to be just as sensitive to light or darkness. It seems to act like a kind of timer telling the lizard's body when to go to sleep and when to wake up.

Brain experts say the pineal gland might do a similar kind of job in our bodies. This time, instead of seeing light and dark, as the lizard's gland does, the pineal gland might somehow be seeing the invisible cosmic waves being sent out by the sun. In some experiments done both here and in Europe, groups of people would spend months underground in caves completely cut off from any sunlight with no way of knowing when it was day and when it was night outside the cave. In spite of that fact, records of when they went to sleep and when they woke up showed, for the most part, that they got up after sunrise, which none of them could see and went to bed after sundown, which was equally invisible to them. Some scientist feel that the cosmic rays stirred up by the sun in the daytime penetrated deep into the caves and into the pineal glands of the pepole, telling their brains it was daytime without their realizing it. As a result, even though they were out of sight of the sun, the people's waking and sleeping were still in tune with day and night.

It is also possible that this single unblinking eye, the pineal gland, could be the center of other powers as well. As it happens, the center of the force of shadow vision seems to be concentrated about where the pineal gland is located. A Russian scientist trying to teach fingertip vision to blind children made another mysterious discovery. The scientist found that one of his patients, a small blind boy, was somehow able to see colors better in his mind when the doctor had him wear a special lens that rested in the middle of his forehead. Strangely enough the best place for the lens was right over the spot where the boy's pineal gland was located.

As we learn more about the other kinds of vision we have or can learn, we may also see a lot of important changes in everything from how the blind get around to how we relax and enjoy ourselves. White canes and seeing-eye dogs may become a thing of the past as people learn how to boost their natural built-in radar and dermavision. We may be able to take special cosmic ray treatments to speed up or slow down our body clocks. When you order food in a restaurant, different music will be used to accompany different meals. There may even be special amusement parks with special sound rooms equipped to generate exciting color combinations and tastes for those with synesthesia. By then we will be the generation of the third eye.

The Power of the Yogi

As a small boy in Holland, Jack Schwarz had read many fantastic stories about the yogis, or fakirs, the famous wonder workers of India. These were men who could walk across red-hot coals in their bare feet without so much as singeing a single hair. They could lie down comfortably on a bed of needle-sharp nails and not even be scratched. Many could stay buried alive for days then rise from the grave completely refreshed and relaxed, as though they had just gotten up from a nap. It was said that these wonder workers had discovered the secret of total control over their bodies, so that they could feel no pain and could sleep underground in a nearly airless coffin.

To find out what the secret was, Schwarz read everything he could find on the yogis and in time learned they could induce a special trance in themselves. Eventually Schwarz, too, learned how to turn on this trance in his mind by sitting quietly and blocking all distractions from his mind. Eventually he got so adept at it, he could switch on his trance in the blink of an eye.

He didn't know, however, if his trance was as strong as those of the yogis, that is if it were powerful enough to block out all pain. Most of the real yogis took years to master the power of the trance, spending time alone in the desert, exercising their minds. Only a few very gifted people learned the secret of the trance in as short a time as Jack Schwarz had, and even fewer managed to learn all the yogis' skills.

One day, Schwarz got the chance to find out just how powerful his trance really was when he was working in a tailor shop. A young girl in the shop playfully slapped him on the chest, accidentally driving into his body a number of pins he had stuck in the lapel of his jacket. Instantly Schwarz turned on the yogi trance and, to his amazement, his pain went away completely. Not only that, as he pulled out the pins from his flesh, he noticed that he did not bleed from the tiny puncture wounds. Fascinated, he took an even longer pin and pushed it straight into his arm. Again, as long as he stayed in his trance there was no pain and no bleeding.

Before long he discovered he had other

strange powers as well. For example, he was able to heal small aches and pains for members of his family simply by laying his hand on the part of the body that was sore. He could also tell just how healthy a person was by studying a glow of colored light he saw surrounding everyone. In one case, he amazed a doctor he had never met before by looking at the man's halo of light and telling him what diseases and ailments the doctor had had in the past.

Being able to poke a pin in his arm with no pain or blood was a sign to Schwarz that he had learned the right trance, but it was no guarantee he was a yogi. One day he decided to put his powers to a real test with a demonstration that would either prove he was a yogi or would destroy him. Schwarz had a carpenter friend build a bed of nails for him, then had it announced around town that at the end of the week he would spend an entire day lying on it.

He had the bed delivered to the town hall and, so he wouldn't lose his nerve, asked not to see it until the minute he walked out on stage. When the day for the demonstration came, he saw the bed for the first time. It was six feet long, sturdily made and comfortable looking except for one thing: instead of a mattress there were rows of dagger-sharp steel nails sticking point up from the bottom.

Schwarz took off his shirt and long pants, went into his trance and slowly, carefully lowered himself onto the points of steel. He knew that if he had miscalculated or made one false move, the weight of his body would drive one of these spikes right through him. Any mistake he made would be a deadly one. He'd be impaled on the nails, his insides torn to shreds, and bleed to death before anyone could make a move to help.

At first there was a gasp from the audience watching him. A nail had pierced his back and blood began oozing out from the hole, but in a second or two the bleeding stopped completely. Unharmed and very much alive, Jack Schwarz settled down comfortably on his horrible looking bed. As a further test of his powers, Schwarz had a 50-pound rock placed on his stomach while he lay on the bed, and asked someone from the audience to come up and hit it with a sledge hammer. Several strong men took up the challenge but both the rock and the man under it held firm. Under ordinary circumstances, the weight of the rock alone would have been enough to force Schwarz's body down into the nails.

By the end of the day Schwarz, completely unharmed, was a famous man in his town and by the end of the year he was known all over the world. He had proved two things: that what the yogis of India did was real, and even a person who was not trained as a yogi could learn some of their secrets. In fact there are now many experts who claim that, with a little practice, just about anyone can learn some of the secrets of the yogi.

A group of scientists found out part of the

secret when they took Schwarz to their laboratory at the Menninger Clinic in Kansas, a world famous center for studying people with amazing psychic gifts. They asked Jack Schwarz to perform some of his yogi feats while they had a number of machines recording what went on in his brain and body.

The one feat Schwarz decided to do was take a long steel knitting needle and push it straight through his arm, in one side and out the other. He left it there awhile, carrying on a perfectly normal conversation with the amazed scientists standing around him, and then slowly pulled it out. The large hole made by it closed up completely and there was absolutely no bleeding where the needle went through.

The machines connected to Schwarz showed that just before he pushed the needle through his arm, something very peculiar happened to his brain waves. His mind suddenly shifted into a certain kind of brain wave called alpha waves which usually only come when the body is totally relaxed. Somehow Schwarz had figured out how to relax his body instantly just before he drove the needle into his arm. Even Schwarz himself couldn't explain how he did it. All he knew was that when he switched on the brain waves of relaxation he could shut off pain and even bleeding in his body.

The Menninger scientists decided to try another yogi, one named Swami Rama from India, the land of yogis. Again they connected all their machines to his brain and body as he performed some of his yogi feats. Swami Rama said that he had total control over everything that went on in his body. When asked for some kind of an example, he said he could make one half of the palm of his right hand warmer than the other.

The scientific experts studying him were not convinced but decided to test his claim anyway by attaching a group of heat sensors to the surface of his hand. On signal, Swami Rama began concentrating and in a short while half of his right hand began to get red and blushed as though someone had slapped it. Slowly the heat readings for that side of the hand climbed until finally one half of his palm was ten degrees warmer than the other.

Impressed by this display, the experts then asked him to explain how it was that yogis could stay alive as long as they did while buried alive. The secret he said was that a really skilled yogi or fakir could actually slow down his breathing and heartbeat and could easily survive on the little bit of air trapped in the coffin and get by without any food. In fact, it was often claimed that the great magician, Harry Houdini, knew some of the secrets of the yogis and used them in performing some of his most dangerous tricks such as escaping from a straitjacket while locked in a trunk dropped in the bottom of a swimming pool.

Swami Rama said that he himself knew some

of these body control secrets and would demonstrate one to show how easily it could be done. He sat down quietly, concentrated a little, and suddenly his heart stopped beating completely and stayed silent for 17 seconds. The doctors standing around the Swami were getting very nervous. According to everything they knew about medicine, once the heart stopped, a person was dead. Without any special medical help no one, they thought, could survive having his heart stopped as was happening right at that moment in front of them.

After 17 seconds, the Swami's heart began beating as quickly as it had stopped, his eyes fluttered open, he stood up, disconnected the many wires attached to his body, and left for another appointment. All the instruments studying his brain and body showed that, just like Jack Schwarz, at the moment his heart had stopped, his brain had been producing soothing alpha waves which put him in the right frame of mind to take over complete control of his body.

After seeing startling feats like these, many people began to wonder just how easy it was to learn some of these yogi powers. Their question was answered when one man, Dr. Neal Miller of The Rockefeller University in New York City, managed to teach some of the powers of a fakir not to a human but to a small white rat.

Miller connected a small electric wire to the rat's pleasure center in its brain. Every time he pressed a button, he could switch on the rat's pleasure center, making him feel good all over. With this pleasure button, Miller rewarded his rat every time it, at first accidentally, controlled a part of its body. Before long the little rat figured out how to speed up or slow down its heart, completely relax its stomach, and even blush in one ear to get some electricity pulsed to its pleasure center.

After the news of Dr. Miller's amazing rat got around, others figured that if a rat could learn how to do all these things, a person could too. As a result, some experts figured out a way to do it by a special method that is now called biofeedback. Since the key to all the powers of the yoga is the special alpha rhythm of the brain, experts have managed to build a special biofeedback machine that actually listens to the human brain and signals a person with a buzzer or a blinking light, when he has his alpha rhythms going in his brain. By learning how to make the lights blink or the buzzer sound, people also learn how to put themselves in the yogi state of mind.

The way biofeedback usually works is that a person puts on a special metal, brainwave-detecting headband, connected to a signal box. When a person starts making alpha waves in his head, the headband picks them up and turns on the lights or buzzer in the signal box. Once the person sees or hears the signal, he keeps on doing whatever he was doing to keep his alpha rhythms going. Usually looking at or thinking of a completely relaxing scene, such as a quiet pond without a ripple on its surface, or lying in the sun on a warm deserted beach is all it takes for most people to keep their alpha waves going.

By keeping themselves in this serene alpha wave state, many people have been able to do some intriguing things to their bodies. In some cases, for example, people who usually suffered from excruciatingly painful headaches caused by too much blood concentrated in their brains would cure themselves by rerouting the blood flow through their bodies. They did this by making blood rush to their hands when they felt a headache coming on, taking the pressure off their head.

In other experiments, people with weak hearts learned how to take the strain off their hearts with biofeedback. By putting themselves in an alpha wave state, they were actually able to slow down their hearts, just like a fakir, and lower their blood pressure.

One doctor even managed to use the special powers of biofeedback to help a women whose face was paralyzed because some of the nerves controlling it were dead. He managed to reconnect the muscles on the face to live nerves in the woman's shoulders. Then, using biofeedback, the woman learned to tell the tiny muscles and nerves in her back to take over control of the muscles in her face. She was able to make her face come alive again using her back muscles and her brain's alpha rhythms.

Even athletes have been able to use biofeedback to improve their performances. In one case, a prize-winning swimmer in Rochester, New York, found she couldn't swim at her best in some races because she unconsciously tensed her shoulder and neck muscles while swimming. This cramped her swimming style so that she lost some races she felt she could have won. After taking biofeedback lessons, she learned how to get her brain to settle into an alpha wave state. Then she learned how to keep those tense muscles relaxed when she wanted. She could even do this while swimming and it wasn't long before she began winning more and more races.

Even with some of the elaborate electronic equipment that is used in biofeedback, no one has been able to duplicate some of the more spectacular feats of the yogis. For example, while people can learn to slow down their hearts, no one has been able to start and stop his heart the way Swami Rama did. Another feat that biofeedback experts haven't done yet is duplicate a special kind of deep sleep the yogis can turn off or on.

It is said that a skilled yogi's brain produces a different kind of brain wave called the delta wave. While he is doing this, he suddenly drops into a sleep so deep that 15 minutes of it is equal to one hour of normal sleep. In one instance, Swami Rama demonstrated another remarkable power he had during this deep sleep

— the ability to hear and remember everything that went on around him while he slept. In one test, a person read off a list of unrelated sentences to Swami Rama while he was deep in delta wave sleep. After he woke up, Swami Rama was able to repeat every sentence but one, word for word. This was better than most people could do while they were completely awake!

Oddly enough, this particular skill is not restricted completely to the yogis and fakirs of India. In northern Afghanistan there is a tribe of people who all sleep this way. Since childhood each person is trained to plunge himself into short naps of this deep sleep for a few minutes each day. These people live tremendously long lives — 100 years or more — and some believe this amazing ability of deep sleep is the reason.

Besides the alpha wave of relaxation and the delta wave of deep sleep, there is one other important kind of wave the brain produces. It is theta — the wave of thinking and learning. Brain experts have found that when a person is concentrating on a problem, his brain produces more of these electronic brain signals called theta waves. In fact, it has been discovered that when people sit in a room saturated with special electric energy designed to boost the production of theta waves, they are able to learn much faster and remember what they learn for longer than usual.

In the future, it's possible schools might have

one classroom set up with theta wave boosters for students who are having trouble studying or learning a new subject. Teachers might even try to use biofeedback to keep track of which students are really paying attention and which are just daydreaming. One biofeedback expert says he could design a special hat with a special sweatband that would be set to pick up only alpha waves, the brain waves of relaxation and daydreaming. This band would be connected to a small light bulb on the top of the hat and every time someone wearing the hat began daydreaming, the band would pick up the alpha waves and turn on the light. Just by doing a quick light bulb check of his or her students' hats, a teacher could tell who was paying attention and who wasn't. Only the students who knew the secret of the yogi's delta rhythm style of sleep could get away with dozing off in class without getting caught.

Others say we could have a lot of fun with special brain toys that use biofeedback. One expert, Dr. Barbara Brown of the University of California, already came up with a set of electric trains which she used to teach patients how to turn on their alpha waves. A special alpha-sensing headband is connected to a power switch which is in turn connected to the small train so that the more alpha waves a person can produce while relaxed, the faster the train will go. The train set was so popular, Dr. Brown also built a slot car racing set that is controlled the same way. With special biofeedback-controlled cars, two people can now have alpha wave races with each other.

There are other brain waves besides alpha waves, and brain expert, Dr. Joe Kamiya, thinks we could use all of them to make music. He says that after a hard day's work, some citizen of the twenty-first century might settle into his special bio-music chair, place a special bio-band on his head, and flick on a switch. His brain waves could be used to play a special organ with different intensities of various brain waves making different notes. If he felt like it, a person could also try to manipulate his brain waves to create special musical effects. Or, if a person was more visually inclined, he could connect his biofeedback equipment to a special kind of large-screen color television set that would use his brain waves to paint different colors on the screen.

There are even some who say that the army could train a special biofeedback soldier, one skilled in using his many different brain waves. For example, soldiers could learn the deep sleep of the yogi that gives them an hour's worth of sleep in 15 minutes while still letting part of their brains remain on the alert. This means in time of emergency, soldiers could get by on less sleep than ever and still be able to perform.

Other kinds of special biofeedback training could teach a soldier how to sharpen his hearing and eyesight by intense concentration.

Soldiers might even learn the special pain-blocking techniques that people like Jack Schwarz have mastered.

An army of people trained this way would be an eerie and relentless group of soldiers such as the world has never seen before. They could march for days with little sleep. They could travel easily by night because of their intensely sharpened vision. In an attack, they would be almost impossible to stop, having the abilities to heal many of the puncture wounds in their body with the powers of the yogi.

ESP School

Like most young men, Wolf Messing wanted to see more of the world than lay beyond the limits of his home village in Poland. So, with no ticket and very little money, he sneaked onto a train that was leaving for Germany. He found what he thought was a good hiding place, curled up, and went to sleep. Eventually the conductor spotted young Messing, woke him up, and asked for his ticket. Since the amount of money in his pocket didn't come close to equalling the price of a ticket, Messing decided to try something out of desperation. He handed the conductor a plain piece of paper and at the same time concentrated his mental energies on the man, willing that the conductor accept the paper as a ticket. To Messing's amazement and relief, the man casually punched a few holes in the worthless paper and handed it back to him without seeming to notice what he had done.

Messing eventually settled in the Soviet Union where this and other psychic abilities made him famous and rich. He used his talents in a show that he presented in various parts of Russia. Most of the time the only thing he did in public was read minds as part of his act, but news had leaked out about his other ability to force his thoughts into another person's mind. Before long his life would depend on just how well he could do this.

According to Sheila Ostrander and Lynn Schroeder's book, *Psychic Discoveries Behind the Iron Curtain*, one night Messing found himself being escorted to a mysterious destination by two grim-looking members of the Soviet secret police. Usually this would mean only one of two things: either he was being taken off to a prison camp in Siberia, or he would be secretly executed and officially declared as a "missing person." (Such things happened quite frequently in Russia in those days. Messing himself knew of a few people who were "missing.") For him it turned out to be neither of these things. He was going to a secret meeting with Stalin, the dictator then ruling Russia.

Stalin had heard of Messing's powers and wanted to put them to the test. The first challenge he had in mind was for Messing to go to the largest bank in Moscow and, using nothing but his psychic powers, steal 100,000 rubles. Messing set out on his mission with two of Stalin's bodyguards who were to make sure he did as the dictator requested.

Equipped with only a briefcase and a blank piece of paper, Messing walked up to a teller's cage, handed the teller the blank paper and opened up the briefcase. Under Messing's suggestive power, the man saw some kind of authorization on the paper and, without hesitating, filled the briefcase with 100,000 rubles. The psychic snapped the case shut, walked out the front doors, and showed Stalin's men the money. He then walked back into the bank and returned the money to a panic-stricken bank clerk, who by now had realized the so-called authorization paper had nothing on it.

The second challenge Stalin gave Messing was for the psychic to visit the dictator at his summer cottage without the benefit of a special security pass. This was not as simple as it sounds. Stalin was a feared and hated man and had many enemies who would have liked to see him dead. For that reason, wherever he was, Stalin was always surrounded by armed soldiers, a highly trained force of secret police, and a group of personal bodyguards. What's more, when he stayed at his summer house, the number of these guards was doubled for extra protection. Absolutely no one got past any of these guards without the necessary papers. Anyone who tried was shot on the spot.

Nevertheless, a few weeks later Stalin was hard at work in the study of his cottage surrounded by all his men, when he heard a voice call his name. He looked up. Standing there in front of his desk was Wolf Messing. Astonished, Stalin asked Messing how he had managed to get past all the men and guns. Messing said all he did was project the thought, "I am Beria" into the mind of everyone he met. Lavrenti Beria was the head of the Soviet secret police and a frequent visitor to Stalin's office. Messing looked nothing like the head of the secret police, but with his psychic powers it didn't matter.

There have probably been many times in our own lives when we could have used Wolf Messing's psychic powers. Well, incredible as it may sound, somewhere buried in each of us there is a little bit of Wolf Messing. Many now believe just about everyone has some kind of psychic talent which can be discovered and developed. These may not be as unique or as powerful as Messing's, but they may be able to perform some of the simpler functions of extrasensory perception, or ESP. After years of experimenting, many psychic experts now feel that ESP is a gift everyone shares.

One reason so many of them believe this is because of something called spontaneous ESP. If two people are very close friends or relatives and one of them is in danger, it sometimes happens that one sends a telepathic message to the other for help. This is called spontaneous because it is not planned and very often the people involved have never had any psychic experiences before.

One of the most famous cases of this happened between the composer, Anton Rubenstein, and a former student of his named William Nichia. On the evening of November 20, 1894, young Nichia was staying in Paris and Rubenstein in a small town in Germany. Nichia hadn't seen his old teacher in years, but what he didn't realize was that he was going to see him one last time that night. After Nichia went to sleep, Rubenstein's face appeared to him. It was horribly twisted in an expression of excruciating pain. The dream seemed so real Nichia woke with a start, half expecting to find his old teacher standing by the bed. Although he quickly realized no one was in the room and he was just having a bad experience, Nichia was so shaken he was barely able to sleep the rest of the night.

The next morning the papers had startling news for him. Rubenstein had died during the night of a heart attack. Nichia later learned from friends of the composer that Rubenstein had died screaming in agony, the pain of the heart attack was so severe. The moment of death was exactly the time Nichia had his disturbing dream.

In some instances the dream experiences of spontaneous ESP bring out even stranger skills than just mental telepathy. One woman described to an ESP researcher a dream in which she actually got a glimpse of the future. In her dream she was going through her usual routine of giving her young son a bath. She left the bathroom briefly to get a towel and when she returned she found the boy lying at the bottom of the tub, unconscious. At this point the dream blacked out.

For some reason, when she awoke the next morning, she remembered nothing of what she had dreamed the night before. Even while she was bathing her son later in the morning she had no recollection of it. As in her dream she had to go into another room to get a towel and while she was doing this she heard an odd noise from the bathroom. Suddenly her dream in all its detail flooded into her consciousness and, rushing into the bathroom, she found her son lying at the bottom of the tub. He had stopped breathing and was already turning blue. Unlike the dream, the accident did have an ending, and a happy one at that. After a minute or two of mouth to mouth resuscitation, the child was revived.

There are ways for people to have ESP experiences without something terrible happening to a friend or relative. Two psychic investigators found this out while they were studying how people sleep and dream. The two scientists, Drs. Stanley Krippner and Montague Ullman, discovered that although the body goes to sleep at night, the brain never does. During a night's sleep it has bursts of activity that we experience as dreams or nightmares. The two men wondered if a person's brain would receive telepathic messages more easily while the body is asleep. With fewer distractions from the body's five senses, they thought the brain would be freer to exercise its own sixth sense.

To find out if this was possible, Krippner and Ullman set up a simple experiment with two people and the selection of pictures. One person was supposed to be the telepathic sender and the other, while asleep, was to act as the receiver. The message was always a drawing the sender picked at random from a box of sealed envelopes. If a message got through it would appear in the form of a dream. For this reason each sleeper had special wires attached to his skull to "listen" to what the brain was doing. When the brain became more active during a dream, the wires would sense this and set off an alarm, waking the sleeper. The person would describe the dream he had into a tape recorder and hopefully the dream would be some sort of representation of the picture message.

It turned out that Krippner and Ullman's hunch was right. People with no psychic experience were getting the telepathic message loud and clear. For example, in one instance the picture chosen for the message was of two prizefighters in a boxing ring. Shortly after the sender had begun concentrating on the drawing, the sleeper had a dream. He described how he saw "posts standing up from the ground" and said there was a "feeling of movement." Generally he said the dream was "something about Madison Square Garden and a boxing fight."

Some of the best proof that ESP goes on during sleep came during some spectacular failures in Krippner and Ullman's experiments. One night a woman receiver dreamed she was in a bad car accident on a bridge. Since this had nothing to do with the image a sender was trying to transmit to her, the experiment was marked down as a failure. The next day the woman learned she *had* received a message but not from the person in the laboratory. During the night her boyfriend lost control of his motorcycle while crossing a bridge. Although he caused a huge traffic accident, he escaped with only a few scratches.

A few nights later the same woman duplicated her first "failure" by receiving a message different from the one sent to her in the laboratory. She dreamed she saw an elderly woman, her grandmother, sitting on the floor in a dark room surrounded by a pool of blood. As it happened, on the night of this dream, her grandmother had slipped and fallen in her house, cutting her head. On hearing the noise, a relative living in the house investigated and found the grandmother sitting on the floor stunned from the blow and covered with blood from the cut.

After tests like these, Krippner and Ullman are convinced that everyone has psychic dreams but few people realize it. This is basically because they haven't trained themselves to remember their dreams. There is a simple way to do this, Krippner says, that doesn't require all the fancy equipment he uses in his dream laboratory. All a person has to do is keep a dream diary to keep track of dreams that could be important. The best way to use it according to Krippner is to follow these simple steps:

- Before going to bed, place a pen and the diary — a notebook of some kind — where they will be handy when you wake in the morning.
- Before going to sleep tell yourself one more time you're going to remember any dreams you have.
- In the morning relax a bit before you get out of bed and try to recollect any dreams. Jot down what you can remember in the diary.
- Finally, after a few weeks of keeping the diary, go back over the dreams and see if there is a single image or situation that kept popping up. It could be that someone was trying to get a message through to you while you were sleeping.

If most people can receive ESP messages when they're asleep, can they also do the same thing when they're awake? For years the psychic experts have said it wasn't possible to control ESP. Someone just had to sit and wait for it to happen. Then, in 1974, a few discoveries were made that changed these experts' minds.

Two men by the names of Russell Targ and Harold Puthoff, both highly respected scientists, had heard about a psychic ability called remote viewing that a few people seemed to possess. Very simply, remote viewing is the ability to see a distant place by telepathy, either through the mind of a person standing in that place or, in rare cases, by projecting one's consciousness there. One man was so gifted with this talent that he could visit any spot on the globe with his thoughts, simply by having the place pointed out to him on a map. Targ and Puthoff thought there might be a few more people who had this ability and didn't know it. They wanted to find these unknown psychics and to do that they started what was, practically speaking, an ESP school.

The two men didn't believe that someone could learn ESP the way someone learns how to add or subtract. If a person had no ESP talent to begin with, no amount of training would help. They did think that if someone had an ESP skill he didn't know about, it might be possible to encourage that person to look for that talent and develop it. And it was on that basis that they set up their classes.

Each person was told what remote viewing was and that anyone who could concentrate could make his mind actually travel over long distances and make contact with someone else's. All each student had to do was sit quietly and describe the images or sounds that passed through their minds. While they were doing this, one of the scientists had driven to a place a few miles from the laboratory. What the investigators hoped was that some of their students would somehow tune in to the mind of the traveling scientist and would be able to describe where he was standing.

In spite of all their training and encouragement, Targ and Puthoff only expected a few of their students to pass this test. It didn't seem possible that everyone would have this strange psychic skill. But that's what happened. Each of the first eight people tested was able to describe the target location, the place visited by the traveling scientist. Some were even able to draw pictures of these places.

At first the two experts were puzzled by the unexpected results of their experiments. They knew there could have been no cheating. No one knew what the target location was until the very last minute. Each location was picked by a tamper-proof computer especially designed to make random choices. Each person tested was picked because he or she had never had any psychic experiences before. Even that seemed to make little difference.

One of their star pupils was a woman photographer, a non-psychic, who had signed up for the tests out of curiosity. From the beginning she showed an uncanny ability to see almost any location telepathically. In one difficult test, Puthoff, as the traveling scientist, was directed by the computer to go to someone's back yard.

There wasn't much to see in the yard except for a child's outdoor swing set with a couple of creaky swings. Back at the laboratory the woman said she could see Puthoff walking slowly toward a huge black metal triangle sticking out of the ground. Eventually he walked through it. Meanwhile in the background she could hear a steady squeaking noise. Her picture didn't make much sense at first until the scientists took a closer look at the target location. Holding up the swings were two large iron triangular supports painted black. The swings were so rusty that each time they went back and forth they squeaked.

Something was obviously wrong. No one should be able to do that well on the first try, they thought. So they decided to do two more things: secretly change the list of all the locations they used in their experiments; and test people who were not only non-psychic, but who thought the whole idea of ESP was ridiculous. After that, the results of their experiments got even more peculiar.

For one thing, the United States military heard about these strange experiments and sent two government scientists, posing as students, to infiltrate this ESP school. The scientists were under orders to get evidence exposing the whole thing as a fraud. A few weeks later two very upset men were back in their superior's office, describing how they had taken these remote viewing tests and had succeeded!

Meanwhile the two ESP experts were having

problems of their own. All their new pupils, even the skeptical ones, were able to do telepathic viewing. One of them was even drawing pictures of the places he was seeing. Their old pupils were getting better and better at traveling around with their mental powers and were developing new talents as well. For example, on four occasions, the psychic woman photographer was able to describe the target place *before* the computer had picked it.

On hearing of these results, other experts did their own tests. They expected to find something wrong with Targ and Puthoff's experiments, but the results they got were the same. In one case an investigator found that the more people he got to concentrate on a single place, the more complete a description he got as a result. All this evidence pointed to one conclusion: Not only do most people have this ability of remote viewing, but it gets better with practice.

Doing a simple remote viewing experiment is not that hard. All anyone who wants to try it needs is a pencil, some paper, a cooperative friend and maybe a pair of dice. The friend should make up a list of 12 possible places to visit and assign a number to each one. He makes the choice of where to go by rolling the dice. Whatever number comes up is the number of his destination.

At a pre-arranged time the friend goes to the place picked by the dice and at the same time the person trying the remote viewing should start taking notes on the images passing through his mind. Because of the amount of concentration this requires, experts suggest keeping the experiment short, about 15 or 20 minutes. They also recommend that, without trying to guess what the shapes and images are, the person doing the viewing should just scribble down descriptions of these mental pictures or, if possible, draw them. Later on, both people should visit the target area to see if any of these shapes, images, or colors can be found there.

In the future, the experts predict more people will be doing simple ESP exercises like this to develop their psychic talents. Some even believe that more and more people are going to discover their extrasensory abilities and, before the year 2000, there will be as many as 40 million practicing psychics in the United States. By then, many people will have mastered the secrets of seeing into someone else's mind, of traveling to distant places by remote viewing, and of wordlessly talking to friends and relatives with only their minds.

Governments will have new problems keeping their secrets safe because this could also mean the beginning of psychic espionage. In one experiment three people were each told to focus their remote viewing on an unknown object and describe it. What they didn't know was that the object was a photocopying machine. Each person saw the machine from a different point of view. One of them even managed to describe the inside of the mechanism and how it worked. Among the three of them they managed to come up with a fairly accurate description of something they only saw telepathically.

By getting enough psychic spies to concentrate on one top secret project this way, governments could piece together a fairly accurate description of it without having to send their spies to their enemy's country. This kind of spying would be next to impossible to stop because it uses no hidden microphones, no tiny spy cameras, and wouldn't require secret agents to assume false identities and risk their lives infiltrating factories and laboratories.

Possibly the only defense against this kind of threat is to have someone with the powers of a Wolf Messing jam the psychic airwaves or do a little psychic bugging of spies' thoughts. Experiments in the Soviet Union have already shown that tapping into an extrasensory message is possible. In one series of tests two Russian psychics were asked to transmit five images to each other with their minds. Unknown to either of them a third psychic was given the job of trying to intercept as much of the message as he could. Of the five images sent he managed to pick up all but two without either of the other two men realizing it.

Even further in the future beyond all this extrasensory espionage, other experts see the threat of psychic warfare. This will be a silent war with no guns, bombs, or missles. The attacks might take anything as their target. Groups of psychic commandos might concentrate their energies to put pressure on the mind of a country's leader and cause a mental breakdown. Those who are particularly adept at controlling objects with their mental powers might have the job of destroying key computers or blacking out communications systems.

There would be no battlefields, no enemy lines, probably not so much as one bullet fired. Instead, the armies of psychic soldiers would be miles from each other, hidden in top-secret underground complexes. There they would sit quietly, concentrating, unleashing on each other the combined forces of what could very well be the ultimate weapon of the future — the human mind.

The Mysterious Glow of Life

The man stood off in a corner of his darkened laboratory. Cautiously, he laid his hand on a flat piece of metal connected by a network of wires to an elaborate looking piece of electrical apparatus. When he reached down and pressed a switch, the area around him came alive with the pop and buzz of live electricity. He stood there, staring in amazement at what had happened to his hand. An eerie glow of bluish light seemed to be surging out from its surface. The light was made up of thousands of tiny fountains of electric sparks constantly pulsing from his skin.

To record what he was seeing, the man had slipped a large piece of photo film under his hand just before the experiment started. After shutting off the electricity, he took the film to his darkroom and developed it. What came out on the color film was even stranger than what he had seen with his own eyes. The film showed an outline of his hand but not in the bluish electric glow he had seen just moments before. Instead what he had was his hand outlined in a rainbow of shimmering blues, golds, brilliant reds, and lush greens, all surging out in waves of light from his hand. And, although he didn't realize it that day back in 1939, the discovery of this mysterious rainbow of colors was the beginning of a lifetime search to discover the special energy of life that caused this glow that he had captured.

The man was Semyon Kirlian, a skilled electrician who lived in the Russian city of Krasnodar near the Black Sea. Today he is known for discovering what is commonly called Kirlian photography, a remarkable technique that uses electricity to photograph a ghostly cloud of energy that seems to hover over all living things — man, animal, and plant.

His discovery was made by accident when he was asked to fix some electrical equipment at a nearby hospital. While he was there, Kirlian noticed that one of the machines, when it was moved close enough to a patient, would send off what looked like tiny lightning bolts or electric sparks to the patient's skin. Curious about getting a picture of these sparks, Kirlian built a copy of the machine he saw and put a large piece of film covering the spot where the sparks jumped out. He put his hand on the film and the electricity left an image of it in a way that both amazed and baffled him.

As described at the beginning of this chapter, the pictures he got were always a glowing outline of whatever he put near his machine, usually his hand. There seemed to be something surrounding the edges of his hand that the electric charge had somehow managed to light up. On black and white film this looked like a halo of shaggy white light and on color film it was a spectacular array of colors. This light seemed to surround all parts of his body, even the tips of his fingers, which showed up as glowing dots surrounded by light.

Before long, Kirlian was taking pictures of everything with his electric camera — keys, coins, leaves freshly plucked from plants, even animals. What he discovered was that *everything* had some kind of glow when photographed in his special way. What was most peculiar, was that this glow seemed to be constantly changing in living things. When he took a leaf from a plant, for example, he found it had a strong bright glow when it was still fresh. As it began to wither and dry up, the glow would get fainter and fainter until it disappeared altogether when the leaf died. This only added to the mystery surrounding this light. What Kirlian wanted to find out was: What was this eerie light that only showed up with his electric camera, and where did it come from?

As it happens, he was not the first to ask this question. For centuries, clairvoyants — people who have special psychic powers of vision — claimed they were able to see a halo of light surrounding all living things. They called this special glow the "aura" and said that it was a reflection of the energy of life. The day someone or something died, their aura died with them.

The reason it exists, the clairvoyants say, is that outside of every living body there is a second ghostly body of energy. Although it is usually said that only a tremendously gifted person is able to see the human aura, some psychics say you can get a glimpse of it if you stand in a dim room facing a blank wall, hold your hand up in front of your face and squint your eyes. In some cases you may be able to see little wisps or sparks of light around your fingertips, showing you a hint of your aura.

The first person to make this aura visible to non-psychics was a British doctor named Walter Kilner. In the early 1900s he invented a special glass screen filled with special dyes that showed the aura of anyone who stood behind it. As a patient stepped behind the screen, his outline was surrounded by a halo of multi-colored light, radiating six to eight inches from the surface of his skin. Kilner said this halo of light actually showed what was going on inside the body and that by studying it, a doctor could tell how healthy or sick his patient was and what kind of illness he had. Kilner said he could even tell if a patient was happy or depressed based on the colors he could see on the screen surrounding the patient's body.

Doctors and scientists almost forgot about Dr. Kilner's screen and the strange glow it showed until the 1960s when a group of American scientists visiting Russia heard about the amazing electric camera of Semyon Kirlian and the eerie, glowing photos it took. Since then experts all over the world have been trying to crack the scientific mystery of exactly what that glow is.

One theory about the glow, according to Russian scientists, is that it is some kind of concentrated energy called bioplasma that surrounds all living things. It's made up of a cloud of tiny electric particles that are always around us and show up when exposed to the Kirlian electric camera. Our bodies act as a kind of battery that charges up this bioplasma. When our body is run down from sickness for example, our natural battery is weak. When this happens, the glow of the bioplasma will be weaker and fainter than on the days when we are healthy.

Here in the United States, American experts believe that the glow is nothing more than a form of static electricity. You can see this electricity in action in a dark room simply by shuffling your feet on a rug and then touching a metal object such as a doorknob or the metal plate around a light switch. If the room is dark enough, you should not only be able to hear the faint snap of electricity, you should be able to see it spark from your fingertips to the piece of metal. Something very much like this happens at thousands of points along the skin in Kirlian photography, the experts say.

Another odd fact about Kirlian photos that no one has been able to explain is that the glow they show around someone or something that is alive not only changes in its shape and color, but it also changes as a warning to a person that he may get sick or even die in the near future. The first person to discover this was Mr. Kirlian himself, when he was preparing his special camera to show to some other interested scientists.

After setting up all his equipment, he decided to take one test photo to make sure everything was working well. He put his hand on the film, just as he always did, and pressed a button to turn on a mild charge of electricity. For a few seconds there was sparking around his fingertips and his whole hand until he switched off the machine. When he developed the film, he had an unpleasant surprise. Instead of the usual healthy glow surrounding his hand, there was a thin, blotchy halo of light.

Kirlian was convinced there was something wrong with his machine and was just beginning to take it apart when he suddenly fainted, the result of an attack of an illness that had plagued him all his life. He was sent to the hospital and his wife took over the demonstration, producing perfect, glowing photos for the visiting scientists.

Totally mystified as to why his machine had begun working again, Kirlian took a few more photos of his hand and got the same blotchy results. The light surrounding his hand was ragged and uneven. When his wife took a picture of her hand, the results were completely different. Her aura, or glow of light, was bright and healthy looking. As a result of this experience, Kirlian figured out that a sick body was one in which this strange glow would be much weaker than usual. In fact, the glow starts to change even before a person realizes himself that he's sick. Just as Kirlian suspected, as he gradually recovered from his illness so did his aura, getting brighter and brighter as he got healthier and healthier.

Some doctors have already tried using this discovery to see if they can predict who will be getting sick and for what reason, just by studying special glowing photographs of people's hands. Dr. David Sheinkin took a Kirlian photo every day for a year to see if he could use the photos to predict disease. One day he suddenly got very sick from a bad case of the flu and was sick in bed for a whole week. Once he recovered he went back through his Kirlian photos to see if there was a sign the disease was coming.

Although he only took a Kirlian photo of one fingertip, not the whole hand, each day, he could still tell from looking at the photos that in the days before he was sick something was wrong with his aura. The light was very faint and uneven looking. On the day before he got sick, it had disappeared altogether.

Since the Kirlian photos showed when the body was sick, Dr. Sheinkin also wondered if they would show when the mind was sick as well. He and another doctor went to a nearby mental hospital and got permission to take fingertip Kirlian photos of some of the patients as they entered the hospital. The doctors planned to take these pictures and compare them with photos taken a few months later.

Two people tested both showed a "sick" aura when they first came to the hospital. There was barely a trace of any aura around each of their fingertip photos, and what little glow there was had a faint, ragged look to it. Months later, when one patient was almost recovered from his mental illness and the other one hadn't, the difference showed up in their auras. The recovered patient's aura had changed. It was now brighter and stronger than it had been when he first entered the hospital. The second man had gotten worse while he was in the hospital and his aura had disappeared completely by the time the second photo was taken.

Kirlian photographs show other less drastic changes in the body than physical and mental diseases. Psychic expert, Dr. Thelma Moss of the University of California, discovered that color Kirlian photos can tell whether someone is drunk or sober, happy or sad, even friendly or unfriendly.

In one test, she had a man start drinking whiskey, one small glass at a time while she took a Kirlian photo of his fingertip after each glass. As he had more and more to drink, the glow around the man's fingertips began to get brighter and rosier until finally both the man and his aura were glowing brightly from the whiskey he had drunk.

In another experiment, Dr. Moss deliberately picked a fight with one of her assistants, then took a photo of her fingertip to see if anything happened to her aura. That old expression about people seeing red when they became angry seemed to apply to Kirlian photography as well, because the madder the woman grew, the redder was her aura. When the woman was most angry, the glow around her fingertip was a deep, dark, bloody red.

The most remarkable of all Dr. Moss's experiments was one that gave a clue to why we often like or dislike people the very first time we meet them. Often, for no apparent reason, we will feel friendly toward one person or feel uncomfortable with another. The reason for this, Moss believes, is that we are attuned to some people and not others, and we are constantly giving off a certain kind of signal with our auras.

In fact, Dr. Moss discovered that each of us has our own special kind of aura that is as distinct as our fingerprints. In Kirlian photographs of hundreds of people she never found two that were alike. In some instances the shape of the light halo was different; in others, the size of the halo varied; in still others, the colors were different. Without even realizing it, we can actually sense what the other person's aura is like and react to it by liking or disliking that person.

As proof of this, Dr. Moss took special Kirlian

photos of the hands of two strangers with their fingertips close to each other. In cases where people later said they liked a stranger, their auras actually reached out and overlapped. In other instances where people said they felt uncomfortable with the other person, their auras had actually curved away and not touched the other person's. One teacher at the University of Utah says he plans to use this method to match up students with teachers they will like and whose classes they will probably enjoy a lot more for that reason.

All attempts to find out where the special force or energy is that is responsible for this unearthly glow have only added to the mystery surrounding it. For example, scientists know that when something dies, whether it's a plant, an animal, or a person, its Kirlian glow dies with it. One thing they have discovered is that this is not always true if a part of something or someone dies.

Semyon Kirlian found this out for himself when he took an ordinary leaf freshly plucked from a plant, cut off a large piece of it, and took a photo of the leaf with his camera. What he found when he developed the picture was not a photo of a leaf with a large piece missing, but of a whole leaf. Although it seemed impossible, the ghost of the missing piece showed up in the picture, completing the outline of the aura.

At first Kirlian thought something was wrong with the equipment and tried taking the picture over and over again. Each time, the ghost of the missing piece showed up. Others found the same thing happens with animals. For example, pictures taken with a Kirlian camera of a salamander who lost a leg still showed the outline of a leg in the photo of the animal's aura. Something of the animal's leg stayed behind after it was removed from its body.

Some experts say this energy ghost of the missing limb helps explain an odd problem doctors have had for years with patients who have had a leg or arm amputated. Long afterward, the patients often feel that they still have the missing part of their body attached to them. They suffer from something called "phantom limb," sensations in which they feel an itching in a leg they no longer have or suffer what feels like very real pain in an arm that is not there. It's possible that something of the energy spirit of the missing body part is still there and every so often makes itself known by these sensations.

While everyone has the energy which causes these strange sensations and leaves the aura imprints on film in Kirlian photography, only a few people have learned how to control it and use it for something called psychic healing. Using tremendous powers of concentration, people with the gift of psychic healing have learned to channel this special energy and turn it on people who are sick or injured. For reasons that are still not understood, this life energy somehow flows from the hands of a psychic healer into the body of a sick person and works some kind of a cure inside that person.

One of the most famous of these special faith healers was a woman named Ethel DeLoach who discovered her powers almost by accident. Her daughter had been kicked in the leg by a horse and was in excruciating pain. Mrs. DeLoach was panic-stricken because the nearest hospital was miles away and by the time she could get her daughter there, the girl's condition would be even worse. As it happened, Mrs. DeLoach had just finished reading a book about people who had the gift of healing by touch and, in desperation, she laid her hands on her daughter's injured leg, thinking she would at least be able to soothe the girl.

The moment she did this, she felt a strange force rise eerily inside her body and move down her arms to her hands. Her daughter later said she felt a tingling sensation in her leg and a few minutes later her pain completely vanished. Soon, word of Mrs. DeLoach's power spread, and others were coming to her for help. One patient who came for help was a woman who for years had been suffering from horrible oozing sores on her legs. In addition, the woman had been slowly losing both her sight and hearing and, according to doctors, would soon be blind and deaf.

The woman had tried all the usual medical cures without success, and Mrs. DeLoach was her last chance. For four weeks the woman went to Mrs. DeLoach for special treatments which were nothing more than her laying her hands on the woman's legs, eyes, and ears as she tried to direct her special psychic energy into them. After about a month of this, the woman had begun to get back some of her hearing, vision in one of her eyes became completely normal and, strangest of all, the sores on her legs had healed completely.

One investigator, Dr. Douglas Dean, wanted to find out if there really was some kind of force coming out from Mrs. DeLoach's hands or if, somehow, her cures were more the result of the power of suggestion in which a patient actually healed himself by believing he or she would get better. Dean brought Mrs. DeLoach to his laboratory in New Jersey and asked her to turn on her psychic powers just before she put her hand on his electric camera. When Dean took a photo of her hand, what he got was not the usual pale-blue aura around her fingertips but great gold and red streaks of light surging out from her hand. The outline of her hand was aglow with an unearthly blood-red light.

In another experiment, Dean asked a woman to come in to have a Kirlian photo taken and also asked Mrs. DeLoach to lay her hands on the woman as her hands rested on the Kirlian camera. On a signal, Mrs. DeLoach sent a surge of psychic power into the woman as her fingertips were being photographed. The picture Dean got after he developed the film showed that the woman's aura looked as though there was another force taking it over completely. Totally mystified, Dean said he had never seen anything like it before and could offer no explanation except that somehow, Mrs. DeLoach was not only able to control this special Kirlian energy in herself, but in others as well.

There seem to be many things a Kirlian photo will show. But there is still one very important question waiting to be answered: What is the force in us that makes these strange, glowing photos? When a reporter asked this question of Dr. Thelma Moss, an expert who's spent years studying Kirlian photography, all she could say in reply was, "We just don't know. We're still groping for the answer."